LIVING BEYOND FEAR

by

Berta Dandler

Shanti Sadan
London

By the same author

AWAKENING TO SELF-KNOWLEDGE

LIVING BEYOND FEAR

First published 2016

ISBN 978-0-85424-069-2

*Cover painting: The Sacred Lotus by Marianne North
courtesy of the Royal Botanic Gardens, Kew*

Printed and bound in Malta by Gutenberg Press Ltd

CONTENTS

PREFACE

The enlightened one is not afraid of anything.
Taittiriya Upanishad, 2:9:1

Fear is as natural to living creatures as the instinct for self-preservation. Yet in the case of human beings, fear tends to overreach its physiological utility. It infects our imagination, robs us of composure, and is at the root of nervousness, anxiety, worry and the whole range of neuroses and phobias. Under its influence, we feel isolated and vulnerable.

The Upanishads, and all the most profound spiritual teachings, shed light on our ultimate nature, which transcends individuality and is not separate from the whole. The supreme discovery of this science of life is that our true Self is one with the ultimate Power of which the world is a phenomenal expression. It is through realizing this non-duality that we can live free from fear.

Reason cannot penetrate this mystery. The truth of non-duality is disclosed to the thoroughly serene mind, intent on self-discovery.

The practical approach to this enquiry and the methods that lead to fearlessness and fulfilment are the theme of this book by the Warden of Shanti Sadan.

PREFACE

Enlightenment transcends sect and school, and the chapters include several suggestions for meditative practice and goal-directed living that can be taken up by any sincere enquirer.

1

LIVING BEYOND FEAR

THE WAY TO fearlessness is to know and to realize in direct experience our essential identity with that realm of pure being within ourselves that is ever secure, ever free from disturbance and threat, and is of the nature of peace and bliss. This is the Self-knowledge that is the goal of the higher wisdom at the core of all the great religions, whether we pursue the path of transcendence taught in the Upanishads, or that of inner communion, conscious that 'perfect love casts out fear'. For the same direct experience inspires the highest knowledge and the perfection of love: both transcend duality.

This awakening to the supreme wisdom is indicated in a verse from the Vedanta classic, *The Crest-Jewel of Wisdom*:

> In the ocean of the Absolute, filled with the nectar of unbroken bliss, what is there to reject? What is there to accept? What exists other than one's own Self? What is there which is in any way different from oneself? (485)

These words affirm our identity, in essence, with that which is immortal and infinite within our own being. When the quest for this deeper understanding becomes our main purpose in life, it leads to the freedom and fearlessness of enlightenment.

Our identification with the mind, and our uncritical acceptance of its interpretation of experience, hinder our ability to see more deeply into our own nature. But if we learn to tranquillize our mind and focus it on the pure ideas that we find in the wisdom traditions of mankind—teachings that point to our true nature—we become aware of a profound inner calm and the possibility of a new and higher knowledge.

Is such a development really possible? We know it is not easy to withdraw our attention from the outer sphere, or to create order and harmony within our thought-world. But if we persevere with our practice of meditation and our enquiry into the nature of the Self, we will create peaceful conditions that will allow more and more of the inner light to be reflected in our mind.

For self-development, we need to impress our mind with teachings that tell us about the path and its goal. We view ourselves as students of this higher experience, appreciating its liberating value. Our deepening interest in this form of culture leads to love, and love awakens the higher knowledge. But our aim and goal is direct experience of reality, and not the accumulation of book knowledge for its own sake. All the information we gather from inspirational sources must be seen as means to opening up the treasury of peace and bliss in our own heart.

The principle of security within us is our true Self. This truth is the ultimate saviour that dissolves our mental and emotional stress, and is the source of wisdom and enlightenment. There is a Sufi verse, attributed to Ali:

> Thy remedy is within thee, and thou unaware; and thy malady is within thee, and thou unseeing.
> And thou art the perspicuous Book revealing by its letters all that is concealed.
> And thou deemest thyself a small body, yet the greater world (macrocosm) is enfolded within thee.
>
> (*Mathnawi,* Book IV, 810-811, commentary*)

These lines refer to the root cause of our feeling of unease, for all forms of dissatisfaction are symptoms of one fundamental malady at the source of our understanding. That malady, according to the non-dual teaching, is that we are not awake to the true nature of the Self. But the remedy is also within us, though we may need help in applying it. It is to gain the knowledge of our true identity and realize conscious immortality.

Through this realization, the purpose of life is finally understood and fulfilled. Each step forward attracts invisible support as we face the challenges of life, so that we are 'alone, yet not alone'. There is

---

* *The Mathnawi of Jalal al-Din Rumi,* trans. R A Nicholson, published by the E J Gibb Memorial Trust, Cambridge, UK. This and subsequent extracts are reproduced by permission of the publisher.

unfailing help from what is highest in us. This flow of support, or grace, may be discerned as the deeper meaning of the following haiku by Issa:

> Even at the foot of mount Fuji
> I am uplifted by the fresh breezes
> That come from the heights.

If we keep mental company with these teachings, seek to know more and more about Self-knowledge, and cultivate our mind in a way that is helpful to our progress on the path, we will gain an increasing sense of security that is based on the revelation of our own inner resources and not on outer things.

This is not to deny our human need for social, physical and financial security, which leads us to depend on outer sources of support. But a seeker of ultimate reality looks on this security as a means to an end. That end is enlightenment, and the worldly peace and ease that may be ours, is meant to provide a safe environment in which we can pursue our quest while we have the opportunity to do so.

Let us now consider how fear influences our experience, and what we can do about it. When we feel insecure, it is because of the thoughts that are engaging our mind at that time. The basis of the higher Yoga is that thought currents can be changed with training and practice. This is not to deny that many developments in life cause us genuine and justifiable concern. Fear, and the feeling of insecurity, often give us alarm signals of danger. We need to have these feelings up to a point. As it is said, fools rush in where angels fear to tread. But generally speaking, our mind gives too much space and time to contemplating imagined dangers and losses. As the writer, E M Forster, observes: 'With infinite effort we nerve ourselves for a crisis that never comes.' Our imagination is a painter of pictures and can easily make a difficult situation worse through fear, while a calm practical response will put things into perspective and enable us to meet the situation wisely.

A story tells of a sage who was sitting on a hillside when the Spirit of the Plague passed by. 'Where are you going?', asked the sage. 'I am on my way to Varanasi, where I shall kill a hundred people.' A few days later the sage was again seated on the hillside when the Spirit of the Plague passed by on the way back. 'You told me that you were going to kill a hundred people. I have heard a thousand people have died.' 'I did kill a hundred people. Fear killed the rest!' The mind is easily gripped by distorting emotions, and then we act out the scenario they suggest, and often it is a 'worst case scenario'.

But there are ways to overcome this natural tendency—which is a kind of self-inflicted slavery. We can learn to direct and tranquillize our mind in all circumstances, if we develop an interior focus. The soil of our mind is prepared, so to say, when we give more thought to the higher wisdom, accompanied by a genuine desire for more light. A point of inner contact or focus forms within us when we habitually practise concentration to uncover that peace and light at the core of our being. At these times our individual self communes, as it were, with our true Self, which is pure and infinite, and our mind is purified by this contemplation. We become resilient to the suggestions of others, and to the murmurs that come up in our mind, for we will come to recognize them for what they are—for the most part, unreal phantoms.

There is an affirmation we might apply inwardly when we notice such thoughts appearing in our mind and getting out of control. Pause for a moment, take a few deep breaths, observe the mental activity, and affirm:

OM. YOU ARE UNREAL PHANTOMS.
I BANISH YOU AS UNDESIRED IMAGES. OM.

We say it and we affirm it, based on the authority of the higher truth within us.

We also recognize that feelings like nervousness, panic, anxiety, tension and so on, are personal states of our mind. This is why we may be deeply disturbed by something, while our companions are at ease. We alone know our inner pain. An English travel writer tells how he was rambling with a friend through some scenic countryside, when his companion suddenly released an agonized sigh. 'What is hurting you, my friend?', he asked. 'My mind is hurting me!' We all know something of this inner condition. What happens on these occasions is that we allow ourselves to be drawn on by our negative thoughts, and these extend themselves like vigorous weeds the more we indulge them.

The mind is our instrument as much as the pen is the instrument of a writer, or the voice the instrument of a singer. We can learn how to withdraw our sense of identification from the stream of thoughts, and consciously direct the mind as we wish.

Take the example of these two expressions: 'I am thinking'. 'There are thoughts.' With 'I am thinking', in the sense of being lost in thoughts, we are for that time identified with the stream of thoughts, enjoying or suffering the pictures that the mind is imposing on us. With the idea, 'There are thoughts', we have taken up the position of a detached witness or spectator.

This principle can also be applied to our feelings, or to anything that appears on the mind's stage. For example, 'I am angry' is very different from 'There is anger'. Similarly, 'I am nervous' can be confronted with 'There is nervousness'. This kind of witnessing—this shift in awareness—is helpful to our mental balance and can, if developed, liberate us from mood swings. For this momentary detachment will free our consciousness from the domination of uncontrolled thinking, and give us a sense of the independence of the true Self.

The spirit of this witnessing practice is indicated in a verse of Swami Nirbhayananda:

In inner silence watch the activities of your mind.
Smile secretly, merged in the divine vision.

What is the philosophical principle behind this practice? It is that we are far more than the thinking and feeling mind, and that we have the power to observe this mental activity and not be wounded or made insecure by it. After all, we are its creator and director. In fact we are taking our stand on the security and freedom of our true Self. This practice of witnessing the mind needs to be developed and matured, as our sense of identity is gradually restored to our Self as the changeless inner light.

Our mind, with its thoughts and emotions, is a source of abundant energy which can be wasted or converted into inner illumination. Ordinarily we do not give much attention to the behaviour of the mind, unless, perhaps, we wish to focus on some project we are engaged in, or need to remedy some disorder. But, generally, we just let the mind go on thinking without any sense of the need for quality-control. Thus we drift into moods, without realizing that we can intervene at any time and give our thoughts a positive turn. Living in this way, we miss our great potentialities for peace, bliss and wisdom that lie latent in the mind itself. We rarely give ourselves time for quietude and for enquiring deeply into the nature of our own being. 'When will we find time?', we say. Here is another haiku, composed by the Emperor Meiji:

> Flitting from flower to flower,
> The butterflies, even, it seems,
> Have no time for quiet dreams.

The point is that our most rewarding time is not that which is spent in excitement or entertainment, but when we are focused on the imperishable truth at the heart of our being.

The true Self is not only free from all fear, being the one reality in all. It is also our greatest support. It is not a support in the sense that the earth supports the mountains, or the sea supports the ships. The ground of our being is the supreme, conscious, living, loving force, the intelligent force behind all the forces of the universe. As such, it is an ever vibrant centre of peace, light and power. In religious terms, our innermost Self is a centre of grace, for grace manifests itself in the form of peace, light and inner strength, bringing relief, upliftment and a deeper understanding.

In any situation, however challenging, we do not have to look far for help. Someone has said that heaven is six inches above our head. It is much nearer than that. The true *svarga* or heaven is in our heart. This is the teaching of the Upanishads. Spiritual reality is here and now. It is the life of life, in the sense that our wonderful human nature, functioning in this vast, beautiful and awe-inspiring cosmos, is a fragmentary and phenomenal expression of the true life, imperishable peace and bliss. And our brief life, at its centre, is rooted in that higher life. So it is not surprising that help is always available to us, because our own being, in its higher aspect, is the ultimate source of that help.

Our strategy should not be to wait for a crisis and then seek a remedy. Let us practise inner communion with our deeper Self as often as we can. If we do so, we will be helped in any situation. More importantly, this turning within will lead to the uncovering of our true nature. We shall realize what we really are: fearless, blissful, conscious of the immortality of the Self and of its nature as the sole reality of the universe. Meister Eckhart calls this great power within us 'the fortress', and it is eternal, higher than the mind, and will never let us down. It is the Witness Consciousness, the utterly calm, changeless Seer of our mental life, above time, infinite, the same in all. This is the reality, and the source of fearlessness. It is our true Self.

2

DHARMA AND ILLUMINATION

O friend, now I am telling you the secret which is
superior to all teaching and all religions, and con-
stitutes the greatest good in life, namely: Do not
deviate from the path of cosmic and eternal harmony
called Dharma, even if it costs you your life, far less
for the sake of the pleasures of this world or out of
consideration for others.

Mahabharata (from Bhishma's dying sermon)

When a man knows the solitude of silence, and feels
the joy of quietness, he is then free from fear and sin,
and he feels the joy of the Dhamma.

The Dhammapada

How DO WE awaken to inner joy and peace, and a sense
of the underlying unity of all? We do so by following
the way of Dharma. Dharma is dynamic spiritual living
—to live in such a way that meets and fulfils our
present stage of development, and helps us on to the
next stage. It sets in motion a progressive awakening of
our higher potentialities so that we advance on the path
of Self-realization and fulfil our highest destiny.

The word 'Dharma' has different shades of meaning
according to context: the law of universal harmony;
righteousness; duty; even religion itself. The Hindus
call their religion the Sanatana Dharma, the eternal
religion, or the eternal wisdom. The word is equally

prominent in the teachings of the Buddha, where the Sanskrit word Dharma becomes the Pali word Dhamma. But the meaning is the same, and is equally broad and profound.

The Dhamma is the whole body of Buddhist teachings on inner development leading to nirvana, and on ethical living. 'I take refuge in the Dhamma' is one of the solemn utterances made by every Buddhist. In the *Dhammapada* it is called 'the path to perfection'.

Religions sometimes give us commandments and rules where the underlying idea seems to be that if we please God in this life by fulfilling those obligations, he will reward us in an afterlife. But Dharma is something vital and immediate. It concerns our link, not with an outer God, but with our own deeper Self, and the uncovering of a light and peace that is usually concealed by our absorption in worldly life.

In the *Bhagavad Gita*, Dharma is called the nectar of immortality, because it leads to the recognition of the immortality of the Self.

> Those devotees are most dear to Me who follow the nectar of the spiritual law (Dharma) as spoken of by Me; who have an unwavering faith; to whom I am the highest (value and goal) and who are ever devoted to Me. (12:20)

The life of Dharma seems to be a lofty ideal, something that only serious students of religion would concern themselves with. Actually, the way of Dharma is as natural as the desire to breathe fresh air and avoid stale air, and what it involves can be simply expressed.

For example, the sage Shri Dada of Aligarh came to know of a primitive community who lived in the woods. They were branded as criminals and regarded by the people as dangerous and therefore shunned. Shri Dada visited the community, and when he stood before them, he sang a short song about Dharma:

> What keeps the heavens from falling?
> What supports the earth? What causes the rain?
> It is Dharma.
> To speak the truth, to be kind to all,
> To be honest and gentle,
> Remembering ever the holy name of Rama,
> is Dharma.

He became closely involved with these people, and he reminded his own followers:

> Compassion is the basis of Dharma and the heart which is not moved by the sufferings of the people around it, is not a dharmic heart. When you approach such people, do so with a genuine feeling of love.

These are universal ideas at the core of all religions, of all true spiritual thought. The same principle is expressed in Blake's 'The Divine Image', where the human-hearted virtues are seen as an expression of the divine:

For Mercy has a human heart,
Pity a human face,
And Love, the human form divine,
And Peace, the human dress.

...Where Mercy, Love and Pity dwell,
There God is dwelling too.

Dharma is not aimed at pleasing an outer God, but entering into harmony with our own higher nature, coming into tune with the Infinite within. Then, let us ask, what is the highest within us? This is signified in the lines of the Japanese Buddhist sage, Kobo Daishi:

The Buddhas in the innumerable Buddha-lands
Are nothing but the Buddha within our own soul.

To speak of the Buddha within our own soul means that the source of illumination and fulfilment is present at the core of our being. This is what is highest in us, what the Bible calls our divine image. It is the essential divinity that is the foundation of human nature. Yet it has to be uncovered, as it were, through following a path of inner enquiry and self-development. This is the unfoldment of the Dharma, which is consciously advanced as soon as we recognize that there is a course of life that leads to Self-realization, and we resolve to follow it.

The progress is, first, to imbue our mind with a sense of the underlying unity of all life, from which the qualities of compassion and goodwill naturally flow.

These qualities reflect the nature of our true Self, which is one in all. With our mind thus attuned, our actions will be freed from their selfish motivation. They will function in harmony with the divine presence within us, which transcends individuality. Yet in its expression in the phenomenal world, this power ever works for the good of all. One who is sensitive to its promptings and obeys them, no longer acts from self-will, but as an agent or instrument in the service of the supreme power, which is one with our higher Self.

Our highest responsibility and most rewarding course, is to live according to Dharma. To understand what this means does not call for a deep study of philosophy. We have to learn to understand the contents of just one book that we always carry with us: the book of our own heart.

As we move forward in life, the workings of the law of Dharma make themselves felt as a certain pressure in our inner being. This pressure first manifests as restlessness. We find that whenever we push ourselves forward, driven by purely selfish motives, we may achieve a short sense of satisfaction, but not peace of mind. On the other hand, if we find ourselves acting in a genuinely thoughtful and unselfish way, perhaps even sacrificing a personal pleasure in order to help, or when we act without being troubled by thoughts of success or failure, we experience a kind of calmness and sense of well-being. Our awakening to the law of Dharma begins when we detect this pattern, which we will soon discover is a law emanating from our own higher being.

The Sufi master, Jalaluddin Rumi, in his *Mathnawi*, brings out this simple, but subtle principle, when he writes:

> When you are aware of doing a good action, you obtain a feeling of spiritual life and joy;
> And when a fault and evil deed issues from you, that feeling of life and rapture disappears.
>
> (Book VI, 3487-3488)

This is the law that tutors us, through our own personal experience, that to harm another is to harm oneself—not necessarily physically, but by causing a narrowing of our consciousness and a thickening of the veil that hides from us our higher nature. Macbeth expresses this when, having expanded his power by harming others, he sadly reflects:

> Then comes my fit again. I had else been perfect,
> Whole as the marble, founded as the rock,
> And broad and general as the casing air,
> But now I am cabined, cribbed, confined, bound in
> To saucy doubts and fears.

These internal reactions are signals from the highest in us, reminding us: 'If you want to be truly free and fulfilled, don't be wrapped up in the little world of your personal cravings. Look beyond your individual interests. Set your sight on something higher, something that is totally free and that will liberate you forever from doubts and fears.'

Dharma means expansion of consciousness beyond self to infinity. As we take our stand on Dharma, we widen our understanding of self, so that it expands beyond identification with the body and mind, beyond family concerns, beyond partisanship with a club, party or country; beyond conventional religious orthodoxy. The path of Dharma will expand our consciousness until we know our true Self to be the Self of all and the only substantial reality.

As human beings we are all endowed with fellow feeling, with mercy, pity, peace and love, with compassion and considerateness, and with the courage to take our stand on truth. But these qualities are often undeveloped, or else they function in a very limited arena. Unless we are instructed in the benefits of widening our inner horizon, our whole life may be spent in the narrow groove of self-interest.

At this stage in our evolution as conscious beings, harbouring, unsuspected, the supreme principle within us, our main strategy in life is to get what we want, regardless of the wishes of those around us—although we often find ways of disguising this motivation. If challenged, we may even feel that it is 'the others' who are being selfish, like someone who jumps a queue, and, when people protest, believes it is they who are being unjust, because they do not appreciate our special position. Our criterion is personal preference and convenience.

A further stage is when our consciousness is sufficiently expanded to embrace the members of our family. But this too can be a constricted outlook on life, especially when our sympathies end at the boundaries of our clan. Napoleon promoted himself as one living in the best interests of France. But when he crowned himself Emperor, he made sure that his relatives were set up as heads of state: as King of Naples, King of Holland, King of Rome, King of Spain, and so on. Whose good was he really thinking of?

The urgencies of Dharma, when we truly become aware of this law of inner peace and expansion, go far beyond limited considerations and allegiances. When we harmonize with Dharma, and continually adapt to its evolving demands within our own being, we shall be led to the infinity of illumination. As such, this great law, working through the human heart, and holding together the whole universe, goes beyond the confines of any particular faith. All religions belong to it. True religion is an expression of Dharma, and has no narrowness whatsoever. There are many who have reverence for a supreme power that they believe underlies the universe, yet do not care to be identified with any particular religion.

There was a rich man known for his gifts to

religious orders. He lived in a place where several religions were practised, and he followed the dictum found in the *Yoga Sutras* of Patanjali: to practise goodwill to the pious, whatever persuasion or faith they may represent.

Once this wealthy man arranged a gathering to which representatives of all these faiths were invited. He said to the religious leaders: 'Don't you come personally, because you will be recognized. You will be instantly identified as Christian, Moslem, Buddhist, and so on. Send a follower. But please do not wear any distinctive dress or robe. Let us not categorize ourselves by our appearance. Let us come together as human beings, as children of God.'

At the meeting, each was encouraged to mix and mingle with others, but on one condition: none was to disclose his or her particular faith, or ask others about their faith. 'Just for once, disregard the labels and the preconceived ideas they give rise to.'

Time passed and people took refreshment, but there was little conversation, and some slipped away early, using the excuse of other business. Afterwards, someone said to the patron: 'Wasn't this unfair? These people are identified with their faiths. What else can they talk about?' The host said: 'I believe there is a deeper essence which is greater and wider than any denomination. I believe the spirit of religion is universal.' 'But what could they talk about?' 'There are many things. The unity of life, the all-pervasive nature of God, the value of charity, the importance of stilling the mind, the ways and means of calming the mind in order to pray deeply, the need to know oneself, the transient nature of the world, that our deepest need is spiritual, that to harm another is to harm oneself. There is really so much we can talk about, and try to go deeper into. To me, these are the fundamentals of religion.'

It was said before that Dharma is dynamic spiritual living—living not according to fixed patterns that never change through life, but in a way that makes for our progress to enlightenment. The truth we revere is universal. And Dharma means progressively to adjust the workings of our mind, so that more and more of the light of the true Self, the wisdom of our deeper nature, may be reflected and manifested in our consciousness, and penetrate our actions and reactions. A meditation text that points to the illumined understanding for which the life of Dharma is preparing us, is:

OM   IN THE OCEAN OF LIMITLESS CONSCIOUSNESS
I AM A WAVE.
I AM REALITY, INFINITY AND BLISS. OM

Dharma assumes that as mental and spiritual beings we are evolving. Our physical form may be more or less fixed, apart from the natural variations brought on by growth and ageing. But our inner life is by no means fixed. The sage Shri Dada once said: 'Do not be angry with your mind, and do not condemn yourself. Your mind is what you have made it; you can unmake it and remake it.' The initial emphasis is on internal change, through meditation and spiritual living, rather than altering our circumstances.

At certain stages in our life, a change of circumstances may be desirable and necessary, but spiritual practice and our entry into the higher life of Dharma, should not wait for this change. All we really have at our disposal are the minutes and hours we are living here and now. If we can learn to convert the present experience into inner peace and light, the future will take care of itself.

One of the greatest, yet perhaps rarest, of qualities, is contentment. The mind is naturally restless, and complaints about our fate, our situation, our friends, our treatment, come easily to our lips, and even more easily fill our thoughts. But a great achievement is to develop the sense of contentment, the ability to remember and count our blessings, and discount our woes. In other words, it is to maintain our higher convictions, our trust, our inner communion, our deepening quest, even amid adverse circumstances.

A Rabbi was once asked to comment on a certain saying of the elders: 'A man must bless God for the evil in the same way that he blesses Him for the good that happens to him.' The Rabbi said, 'Go and see Rabbi

Sussya. He will give you an explanation.' When questioned, Rabbi Sussya laughed, saying, 'I am surprised that you've been sent to me. Go elsewhere— find someone who has suffered tribulation in his life. As for me, I have never experienced anything but good all my days.' But the enquirer knew that this man had endured great misfortunes through much of his life. And then he understood the meaning of the old saying and why he had been sent to Rabbi Sussya.

Part of Dharma is to cultivate contentment, in spite of the bitter dishes that life sometimes serves us. Our automatic reaction, usually expressed as 'Oh dear', or 'How disagreeable', 'How terrible', can be changed. Our response will spring from a deeper understanding and acceptance. We can learn from all experiences, holding firm to the insight: 'This has happened, yes, but my true Self is unaffected.'

How is this inner conviction brought about? Dharma is the path of expanding consciousness. To speak of expanding consciousness suggests that the potentialities of our mind have not yet found full expression. It is the aim of our meditation practice and the following of the path of perfection called Dharma, to arouse the sleeping faculty of wisdom within us. This faculty is lodged, so to say, in a higher part of our mind that is not generally operative. It will only begin to stir and make itself felt when our ordinary mental faculties have been brought to a stillness that is more or less free from desire. If this endeavour is pursued, however imperfectly, the mind will become aware of something within itself that cannot be named or described, but which has infinite value. This higher faculty or dimension of our being, is the source of all the virtues—of contentment, compassion, peace, love, and the capacity to take our stand on truth come what may.

The true secret of contentment is not a matter of will power; its source is the opening up of this extension of our inner being, so that the wisdom of the Self is now revealed and functioning within us. This faculty of higher experience is itself subject to purification and expansion, until its influence fills the mind and dominates our thinking processes.

One's Dharma changes and evolves. The progression is from goodness to wisdom. If we look at the utterances and deeds of a master like Jesus, we will find that they cannot always be described as what the world calls agreeable or 'nice'. One has only to think of the occasion when, at one of his gatherings, someone drew his attention to the presence of his mother, Mary, and his brothers standing outside desiring to speak with him:

> But he answered...Who is my mother? and who are my brethren? And he stretched forth his hand toward his disciples, and said, Behold my mother and my brethren! For whosoever shall do the will of my Father which is in heaven, the same is my brother, and sister, and mother. *Matthew*, 12:46-50

This is just one example of a response that few, if any, could have predicted from someone who was clearly a good and upright man. Yet, when pondered, one can learn to appreciate that such expressions are always based on a deeper understanding, whether or not Jesus's hearers were ready to see matters in a new light. Always he had the deeper welfare at heart, the deeper welfare being the way the human mind can throw off its veils and coverings, and realize the highest within itself, which Jesus called 'the kingdom of heaven'.

For the serious seeker of truth, too, the demands of wisdom and progress to Self-realization increase as one follows the way of Dharma. A stage has to be reached where social convention, the desire to be popular or to preserve our ease and comfort, give way to a courageous response that is absolutely true to oneself. This response springs from our deeper centre, and reflects our growing intuitive awareness.

Therefore, Dharma is dynamic. Its unfoldment within us depends on strengthening our inner communion with the deeper reality. Those who are convinced of the underlying unity of all, and meditate on it, do not need to make special efforts to do good or be good. Their main Dharma is to continue to deepen their enquiry, their devotion and the practices that have been revealed to them. Through this, the Dharma will flow into the outer life and inspire our actions and reactions.

More than this, our practices and way of life will harmonize our inner being with the highest truth, the power behind everything. We will fulfil the Dharma that is right for our present stage of development, and be naturally led on to the next stage.

What is the goal of Dharma? We remember that earlier statement: 'The path of Dharma will expand our consciousness until we know our true Self to be the Self of all and the only substantial reality.' This is the step beyond Dharma, and it is called moksha, or liberation. It is to know oneself to be, not just a wave, but perfectly identified, in essence, with that ocean of limitless consciousness and bliss.

This realization confers total inner freedom, not in an afterlife, but in this very life, while still apparently supporting a human body and dwelling in a world of appearances, outwardly much like any other person. Perfect freedom of mind, yet always functioning in harmony with that higher Law, that deeper reality, is the way of the enlightened.

This freedom from all traces of psychological tension, this enlightened way of action and being in harmony with the supreme spiritual Force, is hinted at in a short poem* by the Zen master, Dogen, entitled 'On Non-Dependence of Mind':

* *Moon in a Dewdrop–Writings of Zen Master Dogen,* ed. K Tanahashi, North Point Press, USA, 1985, p 214.

DHARMA AND ILLUMINATION

> Water birds
> going and coming
> their traces disappear
> but they never
> forget their path.

There is a meditation text based on the *Isha Upanishad* which reminds us of the illumined vision that underlies the great law of Dharma:

OM

WHEN ONE REALIZES THAT ALL BEINGS
ARE ONE'S OWN SELF, ONE IS LIBERATED
FROM SORROW AND DELUSION.

OM

3

LIGHT FROM MEDITATION

MEDITATION is a profound and life-giving practice. When it is based on an appreciation of the wholeness of our being, meditation is a way of progress and inner expansion, introducing us to that inmost ground of consciousness that is free from all limitations and is self-effulgent.

This flowering of meditation will only come about if we treat the practice seriously and as relevant to our entire outlook on life. The methods are available to everyone, but the hidden light and peace of our own being will only be revealed through dedicated application.

This light and peace are not benefits we need to acquire from some wonderful person, place or resource. They are qualities of our true nature and are therefore potential in the mind itself. Through our mind the supreme and liberating wisdom is to be realized. But the mind needs to be guided and made peaceful, and to cherish a longing for lasting fulfilment, before its great qualities can manifest. This guidance is the gift of the higher yoga—the yoga which focuses on the mind and the source of its life, power and being.

Most people are unaware of the supreme faculty of wisdom lying dormant in the depth of their own mind. We constantly underestimate ourselves and see little point in looking within in order to discover a better quality of experience. When we are alone and left with our thoughts, we often feel bored and inadequate, limited and closed in. We seem to be more at home with outer noise and constant diversion. We are encouraged to live at peace with others, but if we are not at peace with ourselves, as tested in our own private experience, what we can do for others might not go very deep.

Little do we suspect that in inner silence, something wonderful and radiant will be released from the source of our own being. For the central fact on which true meditation is based is that within us all there is something utterly serene and fulfilled, and which knows no limitation whatsoever. This transcendent principle is within us all equally. A Japanese verse by Issa says:

> Under cherry blossoms
> All are friends,
> None a total stranger.

An enlightened understanding discerns a hidden bond of unity, and knows all life as an expression of the one infinite life and beauty. None is superior or inferior. At any time, we can remind ourselves of this deeper reality and open ourselves to its liberating power, by pausing in our activity for a minute or two, and focusing on such affirmations as: 'Peace, light and fearlessness are my nature. I am not the mind, which is ever changing.'

Great achievements have small beginnings, and meditation begins as a practice where we learn to sit quietly, turn within and bring our wandering thoughts to a focus, sometimes with the help of deep breathing. In time meditation will become as natural and agreeable as taking rest or food. But we need first to accustom ourselves to its procedure, such as sitting still, silent and undistracted. This self-discipline helps to create some degree of inner space, or inner peace. In that peace, something higher and purer will come alive in our experience, and we will realize that we need not seek far for happiness. The priceless gem of higher wisdom is enshrined within us.

Our challenge is to make our mind serene and sensitive, so that we may awaken and mature our faculty of higher intuition, leading to Self-realization. This endeavour involves seeing ourselves in a new light and guiding our mind in a new way.

The following calming practice, which reminds us of our true nature, may be performed as part of our preparation for meditation or whenever we have a quiet interval.

Breathe slowly, drawing up the in-breath as if from the navel to the spot between the eyebrows. With each breath say silently: 'I am peace; I am peace.'

In following the life of meditation and enquiry into the nature of reality, we are not trying to add anything new to ourselves. Our innermost Self *is* the reality we seek. Our approach is to remove the false ideas and tendencies that confuse our understanding of our true nature. There is a verse* by the Zen master, Kaigen, that gives a hint of this negation of error and confusion generated by the thoughts of our mind.

> The old master held up fluff
> And blew from his palm,
> Revealing the Source itself.
> Look where clouds hide the peak.

Our present mental world, if it hides the truth, is compared to the fluff, and the practice of meditation is like the blowing away of this fluff. In other words, our approach is to remove the obstacles to illumination, and thus reveal our ultimate nature, not to create an inner state that we do not already possess.

At first, our research concerns our mind as it is operating right now. We learn to view our mind impersonally and with detachment—a standpoint that is itself liberating. The secret of enlightenment and inner freedom is linked to the way we manage our thinking processes—our thoughts and our feelings. Uncontrolled

* *The Penguin Book of Zen Poetry*, 1981, edited and translated by Lucien Stryck and Takashi Hikemoto, p 43.

thinking, which goes on automatically without self-awareness, forms a subtle veil over the deeper level of our being, and cuts us off from the inner peace and light.

The first stage of removing this veil is to become more aware of the state and tendencies of our mind, and to give a direction to them that accords with our higher aspiration. This means that our thoughts are generated according to our wishes, and are not allowed to lead us spontaneously into moods or fits of rage or depression. Applying our thought-force consciously is a step towards self-mastery.

The mind itself, including our feelings, is not our true Self. Even the mind's history of experiences, its make-up and moral state, are not our true nature. Our true Self is consciousness absolute and it transcends the mind. It 'witnesses' the mental stream, not actively, but as the ultimate principle of awareness that, like an interior sun, reveals and illumines all. Hence we are offered for reflection such statements as: 'My Self is witness, consciousness absolute, one in all.'

How, then, should we regard the mind, which is likely to be our life-long companion; and how might we ensure that it is a true companion and not a trouble-maker? Athletes or certain performing artists some-times speak of their bodies as instruments that must be trained and treated with care and wisdom, if they are to perform well. Yoga takes this a stage further. It teaches

31

that our mind, too, with its energies and capacities, is a much more potent instrument than the body. Our mind is meant to be an instrument of the supreme power, which is one with the innermost Self of all. As such, our mind can learn to gain a sense of direction from that superior power, and to use its energies for the furthering of our highest good, enlightenment. We want to be truly free, and meditation equips us with those levers of control and insight that will eventually lead us to realization of the Absolute as our true Self.

To view our inner life objectively, from a deeper standpoint, confers a new sense of freedom and power. It is a great relief to be able to observe our inner world as if it belonged to someone else, and to direct our mental interests from that position of independence and authority. We will see, in a way not realized before, how thoughts and ideas, feelings and memories, flow into the mind all the time. They spring from a seemingly inexhaustible source of subtle energy, so that our mind appears to have a life of its own which usually goes unsupervised.

Therefore, when we are asked to concentrate on something in particular, say, a text for meditation, we are likely to meet with interference, in the form of restlessness, distraction or sleepiness. These mental influences are examples of unconscious or unmindful thinking. No one chooses to be agitated or distracted: it just seems to happen.

To apply the force of our thinking consciously means the capacity to think what we like for as long as we like. It is the power to say: 'No! I won't think of that just now. It is a distraction,' or 'Yes! This is interesting and useful. I will give it my concentration.' Conscious thinking means controlling and directing the inner energies. With training, it can bring great alertness and the capacity to spot negative signals in ourselves, like thoughts of harm, and swiftly divert our thoughts to what is worthwhile. A few minutes spent on the following exercise will help us to cultivate our strength in taking responsibility for our thoughts.

Sit in relaxation, turning your attention inwards. Allow thoughts to appear, but when you become aware of your thought, let it pass on by using the following formula: 'Not wanted now. You are passing clouds. I am the sun.'

When we first apply these teachings, we may feel that our mind is hopelessly uncontrolled, and that we have failed. In reality, we have achieved a victory. It is a step forward to realize that our mind is uncontrolled. That itself is a conscious thought. In most of us the true extent of the inner chaos goes undetected, because we rarely look within. In time, given patience, sustained interest and regular practice, meditation will reveal itself as the key to equanimity and self-discovery.

We have talked about the mind and its thoughts and how we can learn to step back, see what is happening and make a change if we need to. The same wisdom applies to our emotions. At first sight this seems impossible, because feelings are strong, spontaneous, and, we may feel, should be left to themselves. In other words, we doubt whether it is desirable or psychologically healthy to control emotion.

But in Yoga, rigid control and suppression are not meant at all. It is more like a rechannelling of those selfish and self-centred emotions that have a narrowing effect on our experience, into more expansive expressions, such as unselfish love, compassion for those who are suffering, universal goodwill and tolerance, a feeling for the unity of all life, and devotion to the one great reality behind everything.

Then how can we gain some leverage over our emotional life, so that it serves our true welfare, and does not lead us into misery and frustration? This integration of our personality is possible through practice and through deeper understanding, matured gradually, not forcefully. This is why in the course of a meditation session, we are given preliminary practices to help create inner calm. Once we have calmed ourselves, and are reasonably relaxed, yet alert, it becomes possible to introduce a particular idea or spiritual sentiment that the mind can focus on and develop. One meditation text that fosters universal goodwill, for example, is: 'OM. I am one with the infinite power of love. I am peace. I am light. OM.'

All of us are endowed with the higher faculty called will. Meditation means consciously using our will on the inner plane—to try to keep our focus and to dismiss distracting thoughts by telling them: 'You are not wanted right now' and letting them pass away. We recall the image in the Chinese poem of blowing away fluff from the palm of our hand. Use your authority as the conscious and superior power that can banish any thought if it chooses to do so.

When we want something badly in the world, we galvanize our will in order to get it. In fact we are skilled in turning a deaf ear to advice that goes against our wish. This selecting-out is applied in meditation when we dismiss unwanted thoughts. Our will is fundamentally strong. It has more power than thought and emotion, as a lion is stronger than a fly. The will is at the centre of our personality. So our will is a key part of our psychological equipment as we turn our efforts to the path of enlightenment, and each of us can plant the seed-idea: 'I can and will transform my mind into an instrument of peace and freedom.' If we occasionally affirm this during the day, we will be strengthened and energised by its light and power.

There is a principle within us which is higher than will. This is our real Self or our real I. Sometimes this real Self—this real I—is called in the Vedanta classics the Inner Ruler of the personality. It is that in us which is truly conscious, and this consciousness is immortal and is the ground of our being. We may not recognize or feel it, but it is ever present. The nature of our innermost Self is peace and bliss. Ultimately, there is only one Self that underlies all beings equally. On this fundamental level, we are all united. Despite the discords on the surface, to the one of deeper understanding, there is but one reality, and the fulfilment of meditation is to recognise our eternal identity with that reality.

So we come to a higher reason for wishing to control our thoughts and emotions. In order to align our inner life with the great principle of universal unity, we need to create harmony within ourselves and, through our meditative mind, that harmony will spread around us without our needing to do anything—without our being aware of the peaceful influence that emanates from our serene mind. As we move in the world, we live in the awareness that no one is a stranger or outsider. In the words of the Urdu poet, Zauq:

> In this world of forms,
> There are a million appearances.
> All are the creations of the divine Artist;
> None is mediocre.

Inner harmony means that all the forces in our personality are pulling in the same direction because they are reaching for the same high goal. We may say:

'There are so many interests in life, so many tendencies in my nature, and they all need their different kinds of food.' But the realization of the infinity of our true Self is the peak of fulfilment. The real object of our love in all our adventures and researches turns out to be our innermost Self. All other loves are partial and imperfect substitutes for the true object of love. Only spiritual enlightenment will quench the thirst of the soul for a love and fulfilment that even physical death cannot challenge.

The true Self is our ultimate source and support, yet in itself is transcendent. It belongs to a different order of reality and is neither material nor mental. How then is it to be realized in our experience?

As we pursue the practices, a latent faculty of higher intuition will become operative. Through this opening we shall discern in our own being something new— something self-existent, self-luminous and supremely attractive. The cultivation and purification of this faculty makes possible the awakening of our ultimate capacity for spiritual vision, called *prajna.* It is through prajna that we realize directly our identity as the true Self, the source of all.

Meditation is thus an essential practice on our path to lasting fulfilment. As a further support, we can help ourselves at any time by pausing in our daily activity, turning within and quietening the lower activities of our mind. This will help us put our state of mind and circumstances into perspective and remind us of our higher nature. We can do this with the help of our meditation text or a calming practice. If we make small and regular applications of this wisdom, the time will come, possibly very soon, when we will know in our own experience that there is a deeper dimension within us which is not of the world, which transcends limitations, and is the source of all fulfilment and meaning.

Keeping alive our spiritual aspiration has been compared to carrying a feather—a task that is easy enough, one would think. Yet how easy it is to forget that we are carrying a feather, because of its lightness. In the same way, the instructions for spiritual practice are straightforward, but they will only help us if we remember to carry them out.

4

THE GIFT OF A UNIVERSAL OUTLOOK

THE HIGHEST spiritual teachings do not belong exclusively to any particular religion or school of thought. They show the way to peace, wisdom and enlightenment that is available to all. The great way opens within us when we are prepared to pacify, harmonize and illumine our mind. The process of self-awakening is indicated by those who have realized the supreme immortal truth as the very nature of their innermost Self.

Adhyatma Yoga is a traditional path of self-unfoldment that leads to enlightenment. Wherever we find techniques aimed at self-discovery through training and transforming the mind, and transcending narrow egoity, one could say that a form of this Yoga is being practised, though it may be called by other names.

When the great sage and founder of the Sikh religion, Guru Nanak, lay dying, we are told that he was attended by both Muslim and Hindu disciples. The Muslims asked if he wished his body to be buried, the Hindus if he wished to be cremated. He said: 'Quarrel not! Let Hindus bring flowers and place them on one side of the body; let Muslims bring flowers and place them on the other side. Then let each group do what it likes. But keep the flowers fresh!'

What are the flowers that must be kept fresh? Those of faith, love and spiritual aspiration. These are flowers that will fade if we do not tend to them; they will fade, without our even being aware that they have faded. They are the flowers that are being cultivated, or perhaps starved, within our own heart.

This story about Guru Nanak indicates that the inner work of self-regeneration is more important than the outer adherence to rites and ceremonies. It also signifies the essential inner unity of two outwardly different religions, and that happiness and peace will ensue, for ourselves and society, if we focus on that which unites, not on that which divides. Thus we shall find that in their deepest and highest teachings, all religions are aids to spiritual awakening.

Then what is religion? The enlightened view of religion and its purpose makes it clear that true religion leads to expansion of our consciousness from narrowness to universality, and has nothing to do with adhering to a rigid stance in which we feel 'I am right and anyone who does not follow my way is wrong and worthy of condemnation.' Here are some words of Swami Rama Tirtha, written around 1905, which breathe the true spirit and purpose of religion:

Religion is that advanced stage of mind in which peace, felicity, spiritual bliss, *sattva-guna* (truth, equanimity and cheerfulness), large-heartedness, universal love, power and knowledge of Self become spontaneous and natural... Our thoughts, words and deeds will not remain tied to the limitations of our body, mind and intellect. These will be free in consonance with our unlimited universal Self.

Religion should help us directly to experience the true reality behind all names and forms in the universe. If we take religion to mean what is stated above, it is the final goal of the creation and existence of the universe.

Religion is concerned with our inner spiritual state, what Swami Rama calls 'an advanced stage of mind'. In a sense, the vision of unity is natural to us. To a small child, there are no insiders or outsiders. But then the mind may be pressed into a mould. We may be told that our reverence and interest should be confined to our own religion, and no other. We may even become suspicious and defensive as regards those who are outside the fold. In contrast to that calm, cheerful, clear-sighted frame of mind, lit by the inner experience which knows that all true religions spring from the same source, the intellect becomes agitated, aggressive and divisive, and its higher evolution is delayed.

To remedy this narrowing of our consciousness, the intellect needs to know how to calm down and make its outlook open, unitive and universal. One can love one's own religion, and yet still appreciate the beauty and truth found in other expressions of faith. This is surely the way forward for humanity, as well as for our own personal enlightenment.

An 'advanced stage of mind' does not arise spontaneously. We have to work for it. This development calls for one-pointed interest and application. Our one-pointedness works on two levels. First, our life generally must be in harmony with our aspiration. Our supreme interest, what we think about most and read about, has to be the path to enlightenment. This should be where our mind wishes to turn whenever there is a free moment.

The field of illumined wisdom is replete with great and transformative thoughts. When, through assimilation, we make these our own personal thoughts, they will lead to that expansion of consciousness where we apprehend the underlying unity of all.

As regards this general sense of having a purpose in life, a spiritual drive or motive power, Jesus told the story of the treasure buried in a field. When a man learned about the presence of this treasure, he sold all his goods and bought the field, so that he could devote himself one-pointedly to the task of unearthing the hidden wealth. This intense interest and priority is needed for ultimate success in the quest for true freedom, which is concerned with the treasure enshrined within our own heart. As our interest is, as our love is, so will our capacities develop, and this dedication will open up the faculty of spiritual intuition.

The other function of one-pointedness is a more inward one. It concerns the state of our concentration at any given moment. Some find it hard to concentrate on anything for long, and constantly need diversion and fresh stimuli. But concentration is a matter of training, or re-training. We concentrate quite naturally on what we desire. We have to concentrate on matters to do with our work. And we can also learn how to give one-pointed attention to that which is highest in our own being.

Initially, spiritual concentration is to focus our mind on something that stands for the ultimate truth, the truth about our own Self. It starts with interest, and interest must grow into love. Love is the easiest way to concentrate the mind. There is great beauty in the world's spiritual teachings, with their liberating message that the supreme treasure is present in our own heart. It may take a skilled eye to detect that beauty, or it may dawn on us in the midst of a life of outer quest, as with St Augustine, who said: 'Late have I come to love Thee, O beauty, so ancient and so new.' It is more than earthly beauty. All the beauty of nature is a fragmentary glimpse of that supreme beauty, the beauty of the truth that underlies nature. So one can come to love these awakening teachings and what they stand for.

At any time, we can hold in our mind certain thoughts, or visualize certain forms that will help to awaken this recognition. It can be a form of an enlightened master or an incarnation of God. We may choose a symbol of equanimity, like the statue of the Buddha. Or we may focus on words which spring from the ultimate experience, such as a traditional text for meditation, or the holy syllable OM. But our object of concentration must point to that supreme realm of purity, unity and untaintability, and be free from the associations of this world and the agitation and desire that worldly thoughts arouse in our mind.

The potentiality for higher wisdom is latent in our intellect. The process of awakening this wisdom is to train our mind to withdraw its attention from the outer world whenever we wish, and to converge its energies on the higher quest. Thus we prepare the way so that the perfection and infinitude of our source will be reflected in the highest part of our mind.

In the writings of Jalaluddin Rumi we find the following lines:

> The gold, (which is) your intelligence, is in fragments. How should I set the stamp of the die upon clippings? Your intelligence is distributed over a hundred important affairs, over thousands of desires and great matters and small.
> You must unite the (scattered) parts by means of love... When you become united, grain by grain, then it is possible to stamp on you the King's die;...
> The King will make of you a cup of gold.
>
> (*Mathnawi*, Book IV, 3287-3291)

Our human intelligence is far more precious than gold, because of its potentiality for Self-realization. But to actualise this potentiality, the contents and interests of our intellect need to be harmonized and unified, so that the divine ground of our being may be revealed. Without this unification, our widely spread interests are like tiny scattered bits of gold, that are of limited value unless they are gathered together and made one. The supreme power is our own higher Self. This power will illumine our intelligence. The mind will recognize that its essence is the supreme reality. It will become, so to say, a cup of gold, that is, an instrument at one with its source.

The same idea is indicated in the saying of Jesus, in his Sermon on the Mount: 'If your eye be single, your body will be full of light.'

Another great universal teaching found in all true schools of higher wisdom, is that the time to practise and clarify our aspiration is here and now. 'Work', said Jesus, 'while the daylight is with you, for when the night comes, no man can work.' It means to take advantage of our opportunities for self-transformation while we still have strength and vigour to act, and while those teachings are available to us; for who knows, our circumstances may change and the source of spiritual food may not be so easily attainable.

The secret of life is hidden in the reality of the present moment, and Self-realization is not concerned with forward-planning, but with immediate recognition here and now. Therefore, let us be alert, holding our mind in readiness to practise inner communion and right identification.

This idea is indicated in a story about the Taoist master, Lao Tzu. It is said that he was travelling to a certain city on horseback with an attendant. Seeing the city in the distance, the attendant grew excited and spurred his horse forwards. Doesn't this happen to us sometimes when we near our destination or the completion of some task? We find our mind races ahead. Our mind is no longer here; it is 'there'. But the sage carried on riding slowly, and called back the attendant, saying: 'Here too it is good.'

This realization of the divinity manifest in this very moment also comes in the *Song of Meditation* by the Zen master, Hakuin.

> Not knowing it is near, they seek it afar.
> What a pity!
> This very place is the Pure Land paradise.
> This very body the Buddha.

Effective practice always carries this sense of discovering what is immediate in our experience here and now, of breaking the habit of living in the future or the past. We have to draw on the treasures that are available to us at this moment, through linking up with the timeless reality by means of our thought and memory.

A variation on this theme is set out in the writings of Chuang Tzu. A fish, called a gudgeon, was stranded. Its river had dried up and it desperately needed a source of water. It begged a passer-by for help. 'Just a dipper of water, and I'll be able to stay alive.' Chuang Tzu, who puts himself in the somewhat unflattering role of the passer-by, responded: 'Yes, yes, I'd love to help you. And I will. Before long, I'll be going south. I'll ask the King to dam the Western river, so that it may flow your way.' 'Oh dear', said the gudgeon, 'I've lost my element. I've nowhere to go. If you give me an answer like that, you might as well string me up in the dried fish shop.'

One meaning is that when help is needed, give it straight away, however modest our contribution may be. It does not help to make high-sounding promises for the future when the person needs help right now. But there is also an inner meaning to this story of need and desperation. We too are thirsting for the water of immortality, drying up in the parched atmosphere of worldliness, which is not our true element. Let us seek that true water of life right away, and not in some hypothetical tomorrow, and then we will have the light and delight that will satisfy our soul. In the metaphor of Jesus, we will drink the water of immortality.

Knowledge of the Self has been called the greatest gain. But is it a gain? This supreme knowledge subsists at the core of our being, unhindered and without limitation. It has, as it were, to be uncovered. No person is without this immutable basis, none is essentially different from it. Ultimate reality is realized as immediate and direct, for it is the Self within all. The mind itself is, so to say, an outer covering of this innermost Self. In the *Brihadaranyaka Upanishad*, there is a series of verses that affirm the divine presence permeating all our human faculties, whether it is recognized or not. Here is one such verse indicating the relationship between the mind and the imperishable reality present in the mind, yet transcending it.

He who dwells in the mind, and is within it*, whom the mind does not know, whose body the mind is, who controls the mind from within, he is the Inner Ruler, your own immortal Self. (3:7:20)

Self-realization cures the hunger and restlessness of our soul. When this Self is apparently unrealized, our individualized consciousness becomes impatient of restrictions and limitations, and conceives the desire to realize its true infinite Being. But because the Self is seemingly identified with the mind, we get confused, and need guidance in how to progress.

The way of Self-realization may be seen as a process of uncovering, a removal of the psychological material which seems to enclose and hide our true nature. The

* 'and is within it' i.e. as the mind's permanent, all-pervading essence.

48

analogy with sculpture is taken up by the Christian mystic, Meister Eckhart, in his sermon 'The Aristocrat':

> When an artist makes a sculpture out of wood or stone, he does not put his idea into the wood, but rather he chips away the material that has been hiding it. He does not impart something to the wood, but cuts the covering away, and removes the tarnish, so that what was hidden there may shine. This is the 'treasure hid in the field' of which our Lord speaks in the Gospel.*

We do not need to add anything to our nature, for our true Self is eternally perfect and transcendent, free and fulfilled. The process is rather one of elimination and refinement—the elimination of those tendencies in our make-up that are based on narrow self-assertion, on *rajas*, on the seeing and insisting on differences, and expressing ourselves in terms of love and hate. The mind itself is to be refined so that its *sattvic* potentiality is brought to predominance, leading to 'that advanced stage of mind in which peace, felicity, spiritual bliss, *sattva-guna*, large-heartedness, universal love, power and knowledge of Self become spontaneous and natural.'

Then what is this Self that is to be known, to be

* *Meister Eckhart*, trans. R B Blakney, Harper & Row, New York, 1941, p 77.

realized—that supreme reality, immediate and direct, and is our Self which is within all? Are there many selves, as there are bodies? Are there many separate souls, like so many divine images, so many beautiful sculptures to be uncovered, each representing an individual person?

If we consider the human body, we find that it is comprised of something like a hundred trillion cells. All these cells, despite their different functions, belong to the same organism. In a similar way, the whole universe appears to be composed of innumerable entities, each seemingly separate from the others. Yet the Upanishad declares: 'This is your Self which is within all'—that is, it is the same Self underlying all phenomena. This supreme Self is subtle and universal; it is not partitioned by anything inner or outer, because it wears all forms, whether minute as atoms, or vast as suns, as phenomenal garments that in no way touch or limit its essential non-dual nature.

What are the implications of realizing this truth in immediate experience? Here is a story told by Swami Rama Tirtha. A dog once strayed into a house of mirrors. It was struck by alarm. On all sides, it saw other dogs, rivals and competitors. It growled, and above and below, all the dogs growled back. It barked, and the others returned the compliment. It jumped about in panic. In the end the poor dog collapsed in exhaustion and terror.

Later, a prince entered the house of mirrors. He was pleased to see his image multiplied. He enjoyed looking at his features and his immaculate clothing. The house of mirrors was a terror for the dog, a matter of joy or sport for the prince. The dog did not understand that all the images were reflections of its own form, whereas the prince knew this fact. Swami Rama Tirtha concludes:

> It is only when we know that there is only one Self and that all the shapes and forms we see under the various names are really our Self, that there is rest; otherwise, it is like the case of the dog. We are afraid: this one is going to deceive us; that one is going to harm us; the other one is going to take something from us, and there is a continual struggle against the forms which we imagine to be different. But once we realize the truth, we know that nothing can deceive the Self, for it is immutable and free.

Our life has at its core the infinite light of consciousness absolute, and this light can be realized in this life. Therefore we are advised to end the restless outer quest for happiness and freedom, learn to still the agitated mind, and explore the depth of our own being. This way is common to all the great paths to enlightenment, through which we may thin and eventually remove the inner veils that appear to stand between us and the perfect happiness, peace and fearlessness of Self-realization.

Lasting happiness does not depend on outer supports. It is the result of being established in peace of mind through our knowledge that one reality underlies and makes possible all experience. To turn in this direction, to make efforts on this path, is to gain nothing but good, and in time we will realize in our own experience how fortunate we are to have been brought into touch with these teachings.

Let us close by meditating on a truth expressed here in the words of Christ. It is a universal message because the same principle is at the heart of all the great traditions.

Blessed are the pure in heart, for they shall see God.

5

THE PATH OF LIGHT

THE PATH OF LIGHT is the way of progress that leads to spiritual enlightenment. There are many traditional paths—traditional, because they are guarded and passed on by those who have themselves realized the goal. The paths may differ in detail, expression and symbol; but all involve the pacification of the mind, the purification of its longings, and its focusing on the immutable principle that underlies our inner life. In Adhyatma Yoga, the Yoga of Self-Knowledge, this principle is identified as our true Self, and the goal of its path is Self-realization. The path leads to the deepening and expansion of our awareness until we know directly the Self to be 'infinite consciousness, self-evident, beyond destruction, enlightening all bodies equally, ever shining'. (*Avadhut Gita*, 1:11)

We already know the Self in a general way, as our essential being or existence, and as the consciousness that makes possible all our knowing. This is the 'I am' and 'I am aware' that underlies all our experience. But we do not realize the infinite nature of the 'I', nor its freedom from all sufferings, and hence its blissfulness. Following the path of light, these limitations of human understanding are transcended and the Self is realized as it is in truth.

THE PATH OF LIGHT

The path leads to the realization that the conscious principle that reveals our personal experience, both sensory and psychological, is not intrinsically different from the supreme and universal light of consciousness. As the *Bhagavad Gita* expresses it:

> The Light even of lights, That is said to be beyond darkness. Knowledge, the Knowable, the Goal of knowledge, It abides in the heart of everyone. (13:17)

In this verse, the ultimate reality is spoken of as light—the Light even of lights, and this light is present in the heart of everyone. Therefore this highest truth, this great light, is not separate from human experience. But something seems to be preventing its full expression and realization. So this light is also spoken of as a goal: the goal of all knowledge. It is already present, yet has to be reached, like a goal not yet achieved.

The verse also speaks of darkness, and the light is said to be beyond it. The reference is to our inner darkness—of being in the dark mentally and spiritually, of not seeing the light. The same metaphor is found in the *Gospel of St John* (1:5): 'The light shines in the darkness, and the darkness has not overcome it.' It is called the true light, that enlightens every man and woman.

The spiritual teachings, if practised correctly, have the power to dissolve our inner darkness and to replace completely our sense of limitation with the consciousness of our own nature as 'the Light even of lights', the transcendent, infinite consciousness beyond all sorrow. Hence the teachings on truth are worthy of unique reverence and attention. The process that prepares our mind for this ultimate satisfaction and fulfilment is the path of light.

A path suggests stages: a movement from one place to another with steps in-between and a sense of direction. It also suggests safety. Our spiritual awakening will be delayed as long as we cling to the idea that we are limited and separate individuals, conditioned by our desires and attachments, at home in a particular mentality and outlook. Since this assumption is almost universal and is the basis of our self-understanding in its unenlightened phase, it cannot be transcended or outgrown without a thorough preparation. Therefore a gradual conversion or inner transformation is prescribed. This transformation includes the simplification of our wants, the loosening of our attachments, and a revision of our ideas about ourselves and the world. This is done slowly through learning how to channel our energies into one strong current directed to the goal of enlightenment.

But why should anyone wish to take these far-reaching steps? The Upanishads reveal that hidden behind our small desires there is one great desire for infinity, immortality and permanent bliss. This desire can only be met by awakening to our identity as infinity, immortality and bliss, which are the true nature of the Self. Although we may not realize it, spiritual enlightenment is the fulfilment of all human desire. None likes limitations and restrictions. All want a happiness that is as unmarred as a cloudless sky, for this is in harmony with our true nature. If we desire small things, it is as if we were making ourselves small, and it amounts to a denial of our true nature.

There is a poem by Harold Monro which shows in a playful way what happens to the mind when it is in the grip of a desire. Called 'Milk for the Cat', it tells of a little black cat who gets increasingly agitated and tense as tea-time approaches. Her focus is the cool, white milk that is brought to the table, but none of it, as yet, is passed to her. The cat at first appears not to mind, but soon: 'Her independent casual glance becomes a stiff hard gaze'. Satisfaction is still withheld, as everyone enjoys the tea. The poet writes, in memorable lines:

> But the cat is grown small and thin with desire,
> Transformed to a creeping lust for milk.

Relief at last comes when 'the white saucer like some full moon descends'.

Perhaps this example hints at what happens when the mind is obsessed with a particular wish or ambition, or when smitten with envy. Such mental states render us 'small and thin with desire'. It is evident that we cannot be slaves to our small desires and at the same time lords of inner freedom. Limited desires mean limited consciousness. Only when we can shift the force of desire to the highest, infinity, Self-realization, will we gain the expansion of consciousness which, knowingly or unknowingly, all are seeking. This reorientation of desire can only be brought about in stages, and this phased approach is made possible through the working model of the spiritual path. Such a path is not external, but internal and subjective. It leads from the darker, restless aspects of mental life to establishment in the light and peace of our innermost nature.

To approach this inner achievement, there must first be a strong sense that this profound wisdom applies to oneself, and has the power to meet our personal need for fulfilment and liberation. At first, there is an inner conflict between self-improvement and rest, effort and diversion. Distracting desires tend to cling to the mind longer than we might wish. Therefore, the desire for Self-knowledge and liberation, even if it cannot yet be the exclusive desire of our heart, must at least be strong enough to override the non-essential desires and keep us on our chosen course. In due time, this conviction of the rock-like reliability of the teachings on enlighten-ment will become stable and lasting.

Keeping to the course is not just a case of dogged will-power, although will, which we all possess, is central. It also calls on our resourcefulness and integrity to weigh up situations and invitations in the light of the higher quest and the demands on our time and energy, and to choose wisely. Our choices tell us much about ourselves, and test our sincerity.

The longing of a sincere seeker is expressed in the great prayer from the Vedas, quoted in the *Brihadaranyaka Upanishad*.

> Lead me from error to truth
> From darkness to light
> From death to immortality.

The prayer seeks a final solution to the riddle of existence. It acknowledges that there is a realm of truth, light and immortality. But the one who utters the prayer recognizes that they are not yet established in that realm of inner freedom. It is a prayer for progress on the path of light. At this stage, the desire has become strong, and the seeker is willing to say 'No' to distractions and make the necessary sacrifices for walking the path.

Who is the prayer addressed to? To the supreme reality, the Absolute, conceived as the power present in the heart of everyone. The call 'Lead me from darkness to light' is a turning-point in human development. Somehow the individual has become aware that in ordinary experience there is a kind of hidden thorn which has to be removed. This inner discomfort manifests in the form of anxiety, and a sense that one is missing out on the real purpose of life. Many of the enquirers portrayed in the classics show that in seeking for further instruction, they have reached this turning-point in their lives. In the *Chandogya Upanishad*, a pupil admits that he is in grief and begs for help to overcome this grief. Another seeker of wisdom hungers for that experience through which the unheard becomes heard, what is unseen, seen, what is not understood, understood: the knowledge of the imperishable. These are turning-points, variations of the theme: 'Lead me from darkness to light.'

The path of light can also be seen as a transition from error to truth. Here our concern is with the state of our knowledge. An error is something that deludes our mind, without our being aware of our delusion. To pray 'Lead me from error to truth', shows that we realize that our understanding itself needs adjustment and attunement with the highest truth. The philosophy of Vedanta explains how our error is one of wrong identification, a confusion or a misunderstanding about what we really are.

Imagine a man who acts the part of a tramp in a play. Suppose, through a delusion, he fails to change after the performance, wanders out of the theatre and goes along the streets. Feeling hungry, he pokes in dustbins for something to eat. A friend recognizes him and says: 'What are you doing? You don't need to be scavenging for food.' This brings the actor back to his senses.

In a similar way, almost all the scenes of the drama of life serve to persuade us that we are the body and the mind, and nothing more. The cost of making this identification is that we are forced to share the destiny of our body and mind, with its ups and downs, feeling without question: 'All this is happening to me'. But we are much more than the body and mind. Our true nature is that light present in the heart, the Light of lights. Like the actor, we have forgotten who we are, and need reminders. The yogic path from error to truth involves taking up these reminders, applying them to our personal experience, and negating the false coverings which prevent the realization of the Light of lights within us.

We have seen that the path of light entails the reorientation of our desires in favour of the great desire for liberation. Let us consider some more of the practices and qualities that will lead us forward to enlightenment.

One step towards this higher self-awareness is the practice of self-examination. Setting aside a few minutes for self-examination, we place our mind before us, so to say, and take a detached look at its condition. We remember our highest purpose: progress towards enlightenment. We then review the day's actions, reactions and thoughts, in the light of this purpose, asking such questions as: 'What have I been doing, and why? How much time did it take up, and was it justified? How have my reactions been? How has my conversation been? How often have I remembered my ideals? Why did such-and-such a happening disturb my peace of mind? What has been the motive behind my actions?'

We also need to recognize that the personality functions in the realm of imperfection and change, and that we will not find perfection in it. Then what is the value of self-examination? It helps us to detach ourselves from our primary instrument, the mind. If we can stand back and examine our mind, we are learning to look on the mind objectively, and to weaken our sense of identity with the mind, which is the source of bondage. In self-examination the mind is viewed from a higher vantage point within ourselves.

In the Upanishads, the innermost Self is also called the inner ruler, that which rules the mind from within. Under self-examination, it is possible to say to our mind: 'You did not react well earlier on. You lost your temper. But for the rest of the day, I, your ruler, am commanding you to keep calm whatever happens.' Self-examination means looking at the mind objectively, instead of being identified with it. It also means remembering that we are, in truth, the inner ruler of the mind and can give a direction to its activities. In this way, we can slowly disentangle ourselves from our emotions. For these, too, are transient visitors to the stage of our mind, chiefly fed and sustained by the support and importance we give them.

Self-examination should be done in a spirit of calm supervision, not charged emotion based on remorse or regret. Everything in the inner world can be transformed through the influence of the all-knowing power within us. As St Paul said: 'I can do all things through

Christ which strengtheneth me'. This means to trust the inner light and to take refuge in it.

Essential to our self-examination is the quality of discrimination (*viveka*). At a basic level, discrimination means that we have accepted the goal of liberation as our own, and that we are prepared to evaluate experiences according to the criterion: 'Is it helpful to my path towards my goal? Will it take me a step forward, or throw me back?' Once we get a feeling for this sort of interior assessment, we are practising discrimination.

On a deeper level, discrimination denotes our inner search to discover the changeless centre of our being, and to be able to say: 'Not this, not this' to all that is passing and, therefore, unreliable. Behind the stream of thoughts and emotions is the eternal Self, ever at peace, and this is to be uncovered with the help of our discrimination.

Imagine a bag of powdered materials brought up from a gold mine. Within this mixture there is fine gold of a high quality, but there has to be careful sifting in order to get rid of the worthless dust and grit which cling to the gold, and even hide it. In our inner world, there is the gold of spiritual awareness, which is our underlying consciousness. All mental operations take place within its revealing light. The fine spiritual discrimination can be made only in reverent quietude— in inner silence when our attention is not lost in thought. This acute self-awareness will show that mental movement and stress are separate from the changeless Self and do not touch it. The Self, as the pure witnessing Consciousness, is ever free, infinite and transcendent.

Another quality indispensable to progress on the path is reverence. Reverence means preserving an attitude of genuine respect towards the teachings revealed by the knowers of truth. It is a quality subject to cultivation. Human nature often tends to develop a certain pride, and does not take easily to bowing the head. But through acquaintance with those rooted in this mode of life, personally or through their writings, the quality of reverence, and its transforming power, can be appreciated and allowed to flower. It includes the sensitivity to recognize that a higher set of values does exist, and that our immersion in these values will loosen the restrictions of our ego and lead from darkness to light.

The quality of faith (*shraddha*) has been called the main support on the path of light. The way of Self-knowledge will solve the mystery that centres on the question: 'What am I?' Faith means trust that what the non-dual teachings tell us about the nature of the Self is true and may be verified in our own direct experience. Such faith includes the conviction that our mind harbours latent capacities that will enable us, with training, to recognize and identify with this truth. Faith also embraces the belief that the supreme reality is within and around us, and is an unfailing support to those who turn to it. From reverence and faith is born devotion (*bhakti*), and with the rise of devotion, our efforts are sustained not as a duty, but by love and need.

Anyone who travels in an unknown region appreciates how helpful it is to have a path prepared by those who know the terrain. Such paths can be trusted and we need to keep to them. If we go away from the path, due to some whim or uncontrolled burst of energy, it is easy to get lost and find ourselves desperately trying to get back to the safe path. The path is a friend and a blessing. It is also an upward ascent, which requires effort and loyalty. This calls for self-discipline.

Discipline in the higher Yoga includes a range of inner skills which are identified in the classical texts as inner and outer control, withdrawal, concentration and endurance—all supported by our faith. Their practice keeps us safely on our path and establishes our authority over our instruments—the body, senses and mind—so that they serve our higher purpose. Inner and outer control refers to the life of our senses and mind, and helps us to guide these according to our choice and with full mindfulness, instead of being led passively by our habits. Withdrawal is our capacity to extricate our attention from the transient stream of thoughts, feelings and images, and find peace and expansion in the deeper part of our mind known as *buddhi*. One-pointed concentration is given to symbols of the ultimate reality, leading to our sense of oneness with that which is symbolized. Tranquil endurance is applied to those situations in daily life that tax our patience or mar our comfort, as well as the major challenges we may have to experience. These disciplinary items, along with faith, are known as the 'six treasures', because their practice renders the mind serene, and awakens our sense of the independence of the Self, culminating in the rise of the faculty of wisdom (*prajna*)—the hitherto latent capacity for the cognition of ultimate truth. Henceforth, *prajna* will be our guide on the path of Self-realization.

The prayer ends with the words: 'Lead us from death to immortality'. In this context, immortality has nothing to do with sustained individual existence on earth or in heaven. It is to recognize the ever present immortal nature of the true I, the infinite consciousness, the Light of lights within, and to be identified with That. From this standpoint we realize that physical death produces no change in consciousness, which transcends the process of life and death, as well as the whole realm of time, space and causation.

The consummation of the path, enlightenment, has been compared to an awakening. This metaphor itself transcends the conception of a path with stages. For an awakening occurs in a single step. From the dream, the dreamer simply wakes up. We do not awaken in stages. We do not have to dream that we are back in our own country, our own home, in bed. We simply wake up. There is no road joining the dream state to the waking state. It is not possible, because the moment the thought of the waking state occurs, the dream is cancelled and has lost its apparent reality.

Such a spiritual awakening is possible because the Light of lights, even now, is present in the heart of everyone. And the teacher in the *Bhagavad Gita*, speaking as the omnipotent reality, declares: 'Out of mere compassion for my devotees, I, abiding in their heart, destroy the darkness born of ignorance with the luminous lamp of wisdom.' (10:11) This suggests that a revelation of the highest truth can occur at any moment, provided there have been adequate preparations.

Enlightenment is the recognition of an eternal truth —the only ultimate fact—rather than a change of state. Those who have realized this truth do not affirm: 'I was bound. Now I am free.' Rather, they affirm eternal freedom, and deny that bondage ever afflicted the Self. As a verse from the *Avadhut Gita* proclaims:

I am without beginning and without end. Never was I bound. By nature pure, taintless is my Self. (1:38)

From the highest standpoint of the teachings of Advaita Vedanta, there cannot really be a path. For how can there be a path to that which is Self, which is not distant, and is ever-achieved? It is a logical impossibility. So the idea of a path is ultimately a teaching device, a working model, a temporary concession to human understanding. Nonetheless, it is a necessary working model which, when followed seriously, will clear away all darkness and error. Such a path has the unique property of cancelling itself when the time is right. Its great teachings and procedures, coming to our aid in the world of relativity, have the power to dissolve the dream of limitations, and awaken us to what we are in truth—consciousness absolute, one without a second, ever free, fearless and fulfilled.

6

AFFIRMATIONS OF THE HIGHEST TRUTH

Willed by whom does the directed mind go towards its object? Being directed by whom does the life force proceed towards its duty? By whom is this speech willed that people utter? Who is the effulgent being who directs the eyes and the ears?

He is the Ear of the ear, the Mind of the mind, the Speech of speech, the Life of life, and the Eye of the eye. Therefore the intelligent, after giving up self-identification with the senses and renouncing the world, become immortal.

That which man does not understand with the mind, by which, they say, the mind is encompassed, know That to be Brahman (the Absolute) and not what people worship as an object.

These verses are from an ancient text, the *Kena Upanishad*. They indicate that we have a higher Self, which is immortal. It is the power that enables the mind to function, the eyes to see, the ears to hear. As such, this power is present in all experience. It does not have a form and cannot be thought of by the mind, let alone observed and measured. It is itself infinite light—the ultimate light which makes knowing possible. It is to be realized as the true nature of the Self, and the purpose of life is Self-realization. The poet-sage, Swami Nirbhayananda, reminds us:

> Seek with diligence to know the light of your personality.
> When the Self is realized, the purpose of the body will have been served for ever.

If the true Self cannot be made an object, how can we make it a reality in our experience? Through *reasoning* we can infer that our personality has being and consciousness which continue unchanged through life. Through *scriptural revelation* we learn that this being and consciousness is our true Self, independent of bodily changes and the stream of passing thoughts. Through *affirmation* we can realize our essential identity with that Self, and its absolute nature: 'Know That to be Brahman, (the Absolute), and not what people worship as an object.'

Affirmation prepares the way for realization. How can we realize the Self, if we do not affirm its presence, believe in it, or attempt to make it a reality? Realization is fulfilment, for Self contains within itself the supreme value, bliss absolute. In the words of the mahatma, Swami Mangalnath:

> What bliss—that I have now come to remember that whatever existed in the past was verily my own Self, and whatever I knew was indeed my self-cognition!

Whatever I saw was verily my own form; whatever I
heard, that, too, was my own Self!
I was, I am, and I shall be! Nothing other than my Self
ever was or ever shall be!

(Vira Vijaya, 132-134)

The affirmations given in Adhyatma Yoga are concerned with the realization of ultimate truth. They plant
in our mind the idea of Self-knowledge, the idea that
will open the way to illumination. They remind us of
our goal, God- or Self-realization. And they clarify
where that goal is to be discovered—within.

The yogic affirmations, being phrased in the present
tense, state the truth as an eternal, ever-valid fact, and
hence, ever-achieved. They strike an echo of recognition in the inner chamber of our heart, stirring into life
our higher intuition, which, if cultivated, will lead to
realization.

The repetition of the sacred syllable OM,
accompanied by affirmations of the nature of the higher
Self, is a fundamental practice in Yoga. Affirmations
used by Swami Rama Tirtha include:

OM   All power am I. OM
OM   All joy am I. OM
OM   Fearless, fearless am I. OM
OM   The life and light that shine through the sun and
       stars am I. OM

Such affirmations, taken singly and accompanied by the chanting of OM, and supported by a life of purity and higher aspiration, will give us a sense of the reality and freedom of our true Self.

The identity of the Self with the Absolute is the universal truth expounded in the Upanishads. The word for the Absolute is *Brahman*, a word indicating greatness, immensity, fullness and perfection. The identity of the innermost Self with Brahman is encapsulated in four short sentences, each one of which is found in a different Upanishad.

I am Brahman	Aham Brahmāsmi *Brihadaranyaka,* 1:4:10
That Thou Art	Tat Tvam Asi *Chandogya,* 6:8:7
This Self is Brahman	Ayam Ātmā Brahma *Mandukya,* 1:2
Consciousness is Brahman	Prajñānam Brahman *Aitareya,* 3:3

The Upanishads as a whole give teachings about Brahman, and through the course of enquiry and practice they recommend, make it possible for us to realize that Brahman—the Absolute—is our true Self. Another way of putting this is to say that the Upanishads tell us that we have a deeper Self which transcends the body and the mind, and that this Self, when fully revealed and understood by us, is known to be none other than Brahman, the Absolute. The realization of this identity is the consummation of the Vedanta teachings. Their fruition depends on a life dedicated to this purpose, followed by people who are open to instruction and guidance from the knowers of truth. One cannot have the fruit of the teachings simply through reading books, any more than one can have a beautiful garden simply by subscribing to gardening magazines.

Do the Upanishads themselves abound in great affirmations phrased in the form of 'I am'? One could say that this form of expression is implicit in some of their verses. But their verses on this theme are generally in the third person, not the first. For example, in the *Katha Upanishad* we have the verse:

> The intelligent Self is neither born nor does it die. It did not originate from anything, nor did anything originate from It. It is birthless, eternal, undecaying and ancient. It is not injured even when the body is killed. (1:2:18)

And in the *Mundaka Upanishad:*

> Know that Self alone that is one without a second, on which are strung heaven, the earth and the inter-space, the mind and the vital forces, together with all the other organs; and give up all other talk. This is the bridge leading to immortality. (2:2:5)

In these instances the Self is spoken of in the third person as 'it', although, being Self, it is obviously that principle that is associated with what the individual refers to as 'I'. Nonetheless, the 'I' as we know it in everyday life does not feel itself to be unlimited, immortal, birthless and universal. Therefore we may be forgiven for wondering whether the Upanishads really are referring to anything that we, as human beings, can seriously identify ourselves with.

When we come to the writings of Shri Shankara, the great sage and commentator on the scriptures, we find that the philosophy and revelations of the Upanishads are formulated in terms of the Self expressed directly as 'I'. In the text known as *The Thousand Teachings*, there are many verses that remind us that it is indeed our own 'I' that has to be realized as the Absolute.

> I am without a second, unborn, deathless, not subject to old age, immortal, self-luminous, omnipresent, not a cause, not an effect, completely without taint, ever one and perfectly satisfied and so liberated... I am the Lord, ever one and the same in all beings. (10:3,10:8)

At first hearing, these are astounding statements. But their intention is not to inform the student of an ideal which, though admirable, is unattainable or in any way strange.

> Noticing that the people are excessively attached to the domain of cause and effect, I have written this dialogue

to liberate them from this attachment. It will cause enlightenment as to the nature of final reality.

If a man reflects over this dialogue, he will be liberated from the onset of the great dangers that arise from ignorance. Ever free from desire, he will roam the earth free from grief, the same in all situations, a knower of the Self, happy. (8:5-6)

We may contend that it is all very well to affirm the Self in this way, but what about the mind, with its restlessness and instability? How will such a message get through, so to say?

There is a chapter in *The Thousand Teachings* called 'Spiritual Medicine'. It contains affirmations which speak to the mind as if it were our pupil, and we, identified with the superior spiritual power, are guiding it to peace and freedom. Such verses exemplify the great yogic principle that we can and are meant to guide our mind in this way. This is not a pretence, because our true nature is that higher power—the Mind of the mind—and we can invoke that power to help us bring the mind to peace. Here is one such affirmation:

Since I am not other than the supreme eternal Self, I am eternally contented and am not in quest of any end. Ever contented, I do not desire my own individual welfare. Make efforts to attain peace, O mind. Here lies *thy* welfare. (19:3)

The gist of this teaching is that the truth of non-duality is ever complete, triumphant and self-evident as our essential nature, but that we need to acquire peace of mind as the condition in which we may realize this eternal fact. The principle to be grasped is that the ultimate truth is to be sought and realized within our own being.

Therefore, the summit of human understanding is to realize that this 'I' transcends the limited ego, and is universal, limitless, one in all, yet transcending all. Just as in the baby there is the seed of the fully developed human being, so in this limited egoism, this I-sense, is hidden the infinite I. This is what the *Kena Upanishad* calls 'the Mind of the mind, the Eye of the eye, the Ear of the ear'. This true I is the conscious light and power through which these means of knowledge are enabled to function. The 'Mind of the mind' also indicates the supremacy of this innermost principle, much as we might use such expressions as the God of gods, the Holy of holies, the Light of lights. This is what under-lies every human being, and, indeed, the whole cosmos. The Upanishad reminds us: 'Know that to be Brahman (God), not that which people treat as an object of worship.'

It follows that any remedies to our deeper problems which remain in the realm of the mind and which focus on our life in the world, can only be partial and tentative. Falling short of the great realization indicated in the Upanishads, these therapies and counsels cannot confer complete fulfilment. But the affirmations based on the divinity of the Self have practical validity and power based on truth. They are a means of lifting our sense of identity from the restrictions of the mental world to the peace and wisdom of the self-effulgent power that is the Mind of the mind. This is to restore our I-sense to its ground and origin, which is consciousness absolute.

At this stage, an objection might be raised. Is it not egotistical to associate our 'I' with the Absolute, which is the same as linking it with divinity, with the being of God? Do we not have a host of predecessors in the form of self-seeking tyrants and false prophets, who have sported the same pretensions and arrogated to their egos the power supreme?

This is an important question. The answer hinges on what we mean by 'I' when we make the great affirmations. Our true Self is not the ego. The true Self is that unchanging consciousness which reveals the ego and the other functions of the mind, but which transcends the mind, and is 'one-without-a-second', the same in all beings. The seeker has the task of sifting the false I, the limited I, the ego, from the true Self, its substratum, which is pure consciousness, existence and bliss, and has no personal or individual characteristics. In our perfect being, there is no trace of egoism. No self-assertion or selfishness can abide in this region of infinite light. The affirmations are reminding us of this deeper identity, an identity that we all share. The true life begins when the ego is transcended.

Another related point is that our affirmations of identity with the true Self, contain a hidden negation of the false self. The great affirmation put in the form of the words: 'I am Brahman' (the Absolute) is not a pairing of the ego with Brahman. It is effectively saying: 'I am not the ego but Brahman'. Such affirmations are not boasts, rather the opposite. They are an effacement of the limited self and its world of wants and fears, in the supreme light of the infinite Self. This matter can give rise to confusion and delusion. Therefore, one who knows the truth is careful to lead the enquirer away from egoism and its various disguises, into true identification.

Then we might raise another objection: 'Is not all this a kind of self-hypnosis? After all, you can convince yourself of almost anything if you try.'

As with much affirmation therapy, it is true that the spiritual thoughts and ideas are deliberately planted in the mind with a view to influence its deeper stratum, whether we call it the subconscious, the unconscious, the causal body, and so on. This is done through repetition, meditation and pondering deeply the sentences in question. But there is something unique about the yogic affirmations of true identity. They are not seeking to confer on us a new quality, and they are not concerned with the world of action and appearance. They are to do with being, not doing. And this being is conceived of as an eternal fact, the only immortal truth about our nature, a truth that has become apparently concealed by wrong ideas. This accumulation of wrong ideas is collectively known as spiritual ignorance. The higher affirmations are prescribed in order to negate this ignorance.

We are already hypnotized by wrong ideas, by dreams of hope and fear, by the lure of the world of the senses and their promise of lasting happiness, which is never fulfilled. Yet the ultimate truth is:

> I alone am, ever free from all taint. The world exists within me like a mirage. (*Avadhut Gita*, 1:3)

Such affirmations are practised in order to de-hypnotize us, to dissipate the darkness, to appeal to our reality, to bring us back to our true identity—an identity which has never been lost, only concealed. These statements work, not by adding anything to us, but through stimulating recognition. Something deep within us already knows this truth, and the affirmations revive and fulfil that intuitive sense.

In this world of cares and trivial concerns that overwhelm our consciousness and keep us bound to the surface of experience, the holy affirmations are symbols of that deeper and perfect realm of pure consciousness, that ever interpenetrates this world of appearances, and is its true being. They remind us: That Thou Art.

Why is it that we may still have difficulties in affirming the truth, so that, while part of our mind is engaged in the meditation on: 'I am peace. I am light. I am bliss', other parts of the mind stay as deniers or doubting Thomases, and say: 'You are no such thing.'?

One reason is that we have not truly grasped the fine distinction between the ego and the Self. This is not surprising. Both are subtle. Relatively speaking, both the ego and the Self are interior. Both are indicated by the same word: 'I'. No wonder there is confusion.

The answer is to deepen one's enquiry, in particular to note the transient nature of the ego, and that it, too, is an object in the world of objects. It is not the true subject, and the true subject is that unbroken awareness that knows all our experiences, whether the ego is part of them or not.

Another reason for the difficulty in applying to oneself the yogic affirmations of identity with truth, is that the mind is at home with material things, qualities and movement, whereas the true Self or Brahman transcends form and quality, and is motionless. This is why, for most of us, the Absolute has to be approached through symbols—images or words that have an affinity with the realm of perfection, that mean something to our mind and can be a focus of attention. Such symbols indicate the supreme reality beyond the mind, and when held in our attention, effect a clearing, rendering the mind sensitive to that which is symbolized and transcends thought. In this sense, light is a

symbol, peace is a symbol, the forms of the incarn-
ations of God, or of an illumined saint or sage, are
symbols, as is the sound and form of OM, pointing to
the highest in us. These conceptions, are, as it were,
means to lead our understanding to the pure abstraction
of our reality. Withdrawing into this inner realm, with
the feeling, 'OM I am peace. OM I am light', will, in
time, pacify and inform the mind in such a way that
something of the ultimate peace and light, whose
source is the true Self, will be reflected in the mind. We
will know that our orientation is right, and will have the
capacity to probe more deeply.

It is a mistake to think that the quest for a reality that
is formless will diminish our experience. For this
spiritual formlessness is the complete freedom from
limitations. Moreover, it is within the so-called formlessness of Brahman that the whole world of duality
makes its illusory appearance.

This paradox, of the formlessness of that principle on
which are strung, like pearls, heaven and earth, is the
theme of several verses in the *Ashtavakra Gita*:

> Wonderful am I! In spite of the body and its properties,
> I am one. I go nowhere, I come from nowhere, I abide
> in my Self, pervading the whole universe. (2:12)

> All praise be to me, I am most skilful, I, without a
> form, uphold the universe through all eternity. (2:13)

AFFIRMATIONS OF THE HIGHEST TRUTH

I am wonderful, adoration to my Self. I own nothing, and yet all that is thought or spoken of is mine. (2:14)

There are problems in visualizing or conceptualizing such a truth, which transcends the intellect. But, just as it says in the Bible, 'Blessed are the pure in heart, for they shall see God', so too, as one proceeds on the path of Yoga, a higher faculty in the mind awakens, through which our understanding of truth deepens and widens far beyond the insights yielded by reason. This faculty of spiritual perception leads ultimately to realization.

Let us ponder a short sentence from a text that has the dual virtue of reminding us that we are the masters of our inner life and can guide it, and also that affirms the highest truth:

OM   BE STILL AND KNOW THAT I AM GOD.   OM

Expressed in terms of the non-dual teachings:

OM BE STILL, O MIND, AND KNOW
THAT I AM TRUTH INFINITE. OM

7

POINTERS TO PEACE FROM
A MYSTICAL POET

INNER PEACE is the best remedy for the stresses and uncertainties of life. But how to find inner peace and what is its source? We travel far in search of peaceful places, in expectation that when we arrive, the tranquil environment will influence us and fill us with the blessings of peace. But it does not always happen, because we take with us our mind, which is capable of staying restless and tense however pleasing the outer circumstances.

Another strategy is to seek peace within ourselves, and this is the way of the spiritual Yoga. It is based on the teaching that peace already abides at the deepest level of our being. It does not have to be created or acquired. But a training is needed to uncover it. This training begins with efforts to make the mind peaceful, and evolves into a higher quest. For if we want the permanent peace that will dissolve forever the conviction 'I am the sufferer', we have the possibility of discovering the fountainhead of all peace—the imperishable reality that underlies the mind.

Here we are approaching a region which is neither material nor mental, that has no boundary and is unaffected by time, space and causation. This transcendent principle is our true Self, and when fully revealed, it is realized as the supreme power that supports and makes possible the world of appearances.

It is true that when we speak of ourselves, we nearly always do so in terms of ordinary conventions. We are naturally identified with a particular body. We have a mental life that we feel is our own private domain. And when we talk of 'me' or 'mine', we are usually referring to our personality or possessions. Unfortunately, we cannot say that this personality is immortal, infinite and transcendent, however much we may seek to promote ourselves in the course of our careers. We may, like Cleopatra, have immortal longings, but we will never truly realize these immortal longings until we have learnt how to transcend our sense of identity with the body and the mind, and awakened to our true identity.

Another phrase for 'true identity' is 'true Self'. Identity means 'I' and whatever we associate with that 'I'. Deep reflection reveals that there is an 'I', or basis of selfhood, that transcends the confinement of human individuality and is the essential being in all, the 'divine ground' or substratum, the support of all experience. It is not individualized, but universal, infinite and undivided. Being the true Self of all, its nature—our nature—is the source of all peace, bliss and consciousness.

The first and most important pointer to peace is to become familiar with the doctrine of Self-knowledge —that there is a deeper Self. It can only be discovered within, and this is the theme of a poem from the yogic mystical tradition, which contrasts the inner quest with the practice of making pilgrimages to holy places:

> O friend, why do you wander in Hardwar and Prayag?
> Do you not know what you are?
> He is hidden within the veil of your personality, O Prince.
> To know Him you do not need to travel far and wide.
> ...Some have gone to Ka'aba, but when they return they say:
> 'We did not see the divine Lord there.'
> ...O friend, in every stone His light is hidden.
> He is not confined only to Mount Sinai.
> He is concealed within the veil of your personality, O Prince,
> In search of Him you do not need to travel far and wide.

We learn about the inner peace of the true Self from the illumined sages, rather than from philosophers or psychologists. These sages are specialists in inner peace. There is no one nation, no particular religion, that has a monopoly of this expertise. Some further lines from the same poem remind us:

> He is Christianity among the Christians, in Islam he appears as Islam.

But He has no banner, and does not bear the shield of
any particular religion.
Among the Hindus he appears as a Hindu,
But in fact he has no special creed.
He dwells in every object, but He is a stranger to any
partiality.

This spirit of universality is another pointer to inner
peace. Self-realization is independent of any particular
religion and it reveals the underlying unity of all. The
preparation for this realization is to cultivate a sense of
universal fraternity. If this attitude is taken up, it may
or may not have visible results in the outer life, but its
benefits make themselves known to the one who cult-
ivates this outlook. The main obstacles on the path to
inner peace are the feelings of conflict and antagonism
we harbour for other people, races or creeds—whether
we nurse such antagonism consciously or not. Such
feelings strengthen the sense of separateness and fear.
The purpose of the higher teachings is to dissolve all
sense of separateness, and with it, to uproot the cause
of fear.

The poet whose lines we have been quoting is a sage
who lived in Northern India in the nineteenth century
named Swami Nirbhayananda. He was a traditional
teacher who had received a mandate to transmit the
highest teachings of the Yoga of Self-knowledge from
his Guru. One of his gifts was the ability to convey
guidance through his poems and songs. Most of his

teachings have come down to us in this form. In this way, he would sing to the people in the villages and give discourses according to their needs. Then, as now, there were many popular songs in circulation that stayed in people's minds for better or worse. The Swami sometimes took up the tunes of these songs and substituted his own words, drawing the people's attention to the region of eternal peace and light within their own being.

Having known the ultimate secret of inner peace, the Swami was an adept at detecting the ways people harm themselves through wrong ideas and practices. So he would gently suggest ways of thought and conduct that would let in the light, and remind them of the real way forward to inner enlightenment. If he discovered that a feud or vendetta was dividing a particular community, he would sing of harmony and unity, and of the futility of anger. Here are a few short verses in this vein, taken from his *A Hundred Stanzas on Peace*:

O Nirbhaya, break the quiver of anger. You have no enemy, O friend.
Forgive cheerfully the faults of others, O Nirbhaya;
Then you also will be forgiven.
O Nirbhaya, do not be angry or bitter even with a stray dog;
Your Master pervades both the moving and the fixed.
O Nirbhaya, do not oppress those who are poor and helpless.

Know that the high, the low and the ignorant all belong to God.

O Nirbhaya, be not severe with anyone, nor show a sour face.

Live in peace and harmony, and give up your feeling of self-superiority.

O Nirbhaya, give the same love to Hindu, Christian and Turk.

Renounce the conception of 'I' and 'You'. Do not tire your soul.

We notice that in all these verses, Swami Nirbhayananda includes the words: O Nirbhaya. The fact is, he is addressing his verses to himself, but allowing other people to eavesdrop, so to say, on his call for self-awakening. This self-instruction is a device he uses frequently, and it relieves us of the uncomfortable feeling that we are being preached at by a superior. On the other hand, there is nothing to stop us from using such verses for ourselves by taking the bold step of substituting our own name. For instance, Swami Nirbhayananda had a follower whose name was Brahmananda. So he might well have used the verses in this way:

O Brahmananda, awaken the light of pure Consciousness in your being, and do not play the spy.

Let your mind rest in contemplation of the ever-shining light in your soul.

This device brings the spiritual quest nearer home, because such precepts are only effective if they are taken personally. No one can teach us anything if we are not prepared to tutor ourselves.

Another theme of Swami Nirbhayananda's poetry is that the pointers to peace—which *are* the higher teachings—greet us in life as a rare opportunity which may not always be available to us. Therefore it makes sense to apply this wisdom as soon as possible, for there is work to be done. The way of wisdom has first to be introduced and accepted, stabilized, and then carried through to its mature outcome, enlightenment. One cannot begin such a process too soon. It is a great chance. On the other hand, how long we will actually live is a matter of uncertainty. Looked at from a wider perspective, all human lives are short. So this theme of taking one's chance while one has it, often appears in his verses. Here are some examples, where again we find the Swami engaged in tutoring his most regular pupil: his own mind.

O Nirbhaya, your chance has now come, and you cannot avoid the challenge.
You are equipped to face it in every limb.
Be fearless. Do not waver.
Look on this magic show, the world, O Nirbhaya.
You have a human body. Do not waste it.
Morning follows evening, evening morning, and so it goes on.

Until you know your own nature, O foolish one,
Your work is never done.
The thunder-cloud death is growling
And you have already been spattered by the first
shower of rain-drops,
Yet you continue to sleep, you sluggard!
How do you think it will end?

What is this opportunity that the Swami is talking about? It is nothing less than the chance to discover the source of lasting peace in one's own being. Through this path we will develop capacities that will remove the sting from any adversity we may meet in life, because we will see things in a new perspective. This is the way to gain real wisdom through enlightenment, and the key to enlightenment is Self-knowledge.

The chance arises when we come into touch with traditional and pure teachings about our higher nature and potentialities. This immediately presents us with a choice: hear more, or ignore. This may involve seeking out a source where the teachings are given impersonally and in a pure form. Swami Nirbhayananda expresses this phase when he writes:

Search for the meeting-place of your fellow devotees,
O Nirbhaya.
In their company your sorrows will be over and your
heart will know peace.

Our way forward depends on taking up certain practices, for example, daily meditation. We can choose to exercise our will in order to give time to such a practice, or we may decide that it is troublesome and inconvenient. Even when we have achieved this triumph of the will, we have to think in terms of sustained effort. Skill in meditation matures slowly and depends on regular practice with great interest. As with all creative activities, we need the will-power to establish the meditation habit. Even to stay seated in a meditation posture for the appointed time can be a surprising challenge. But once this initial stage of self-mastery is accomplished, we will find ourselves approaching the practice not only with deep interest, but with a desire and thirst for the peace, bliss and wisdom of Self-knowledge. Our deeper interest and thirst will achieve what will-power alone can never achieve: loving concentration on the transcendent principle hidden in our own heart. Our meditation will be blessed with periods of 'effortless effort' and the practice will soon become an essential source of inner nourishment.

Here is a verse that stresses the importance of practising meditation:

Continue your meditation, concentration and absorption always.
At the time of death, nothing further will be accomplished.

The principle behind this inner quest is expressed in the following verse:

> In the end the seeker finds he is the one sought.
> O Nirbhaya, your love is within your own personality.

Once we have regularized the practice of meditation and are pursuing the goal of Self-realization, we will become aware of the real challenge that faces each and everyone who takes up this higher quest: the challenge presented by the mind itself. When we turn within and try to develop some degree of inner peace, so often we seem to find our mind in the opposite condition. Instead of peace there is tension, restlessness, unwanted thoughts and memories. At this stage we need to be patient, and to be willing to apply some well-tried techniques that will gradually bring the mind to a state of peace. It is comforting to find that several of the poems of Swami Nirbhayananda frankly acknowledge this difficulty. More than once, he begins a poem with the words:

> O my mind, you and I cannot be friends.

Here we are given the wholesome thought that the mind, whatever its condition, is not our true Self. The Swami speaks *to* the mind. He does not speak *as* the mind. 'O my mind, you and I cannot be friends.' This is important to remember. In this apparently simple line, the Swami is speaking *to* his own mind as an object of which he is aware. It is a 'you'. It is not 'I'.

Earlier we referred to the teaching that the Self transcends the body and the mind, and is immutable and infinite. This is a call to take our stand on our true nature and to survey and learn to command our mind from a more inward and higher standpoint. This separation of the true Self from the mind, is based on the supreme truth, and has important practical implications that reveal themselves as we go deeper into Yoga. This principle underlies all the verses we have quoted where Swami Nirbhayananda addresses himself as 'O Nirbhaya'. In essence, he is reminding his own mind of the right path to be trodden, the path of wisdom. He is also guiding his mind away from paths which lead to suffering.

This whole course of self-tuition—of objectifying the mental life and ensuring that it moves progressively —is a means to an end. Its aim is to transform our mind into a useful instrument that will help and not hinder our progress on the path. Speaking figuratively, this process is sometimes called 'making a friend of the mind'. Our mind can become amiable and helpful when it is habitually soaked in the higher teachings and conforms to the right values. In this way, our mind will lose its restlessness and tension, and will learn to find joy, value and relevance in the words of the enlightened sages, which turn the searchlight on the hidden beauty and peace of our true nature.

Swami Nirbhayananda recognizes both aspects of the human mind: first of all as a kind of obstacle or veil, and secondly as a dear friend, once it has been suitably educated and turned into an aid to enlightenment. Here are some lines which present the mind at its most resistant:

O Nirbhaya, the mind is unruly and a bad son.
It strains at the leash and offends against the code.
It works destruction day and night.

O my mind, you and I cannot be friends.
I want contemplation of the infinite
And to serve Him in poor folks,
While you desire ease and comfort.
I am all Light and Consciousness Infinite,
You are, my mind, a slave, a beggar,
Seeking dependence on shadows.

The mind is addressed firmly but from a distance, and not by one who is entangled in the mind we are addressing. In other words, we have taken up an inner vantage point that is superior to the mind. This mode of expression allows the mind to be transformed through this subtle monitoring and instruction. It is a case of affirming what we have already been told about the true nature of the Self, which we know intellectually and indirectly, but which will be known directly when the path has been successfully trod. Let us briefly remind ourselves of the true nature of the Self, as expressed poetically in these lines of Swami Nirbhayananda:

> There is no cause for sorrow or weeping, O Nirbhaya.
> Know that you are the light of the world.
> The whole cosmos is contained in you.
> Without the Self there would have been no world.
> O Nirbhaya, you are the one support of the moving and the fixed.

And again, from another poem:

> You yourself are the light of Consciousness,
> You yourself are Knowledge Infinite,
> You yourself pervade the universe,
> You yourself are the fount of all joy.
> There is not a trace of suffering in you.

It was noted before that the same mind, which at first is our main challenge, can, with patience and perseverance, be converted into our greatest helper. It depends on how we ourselves lead our mind. In fact, a great part of Yoga is to learn that we are the true guides of our inner life. We may need instruction and support, but we soon realize that our mind-management is primarily in our own hands.

In another poem, we find the Swami congratulating his mind on the wise choices it applied in helping his progress to Self-knowledge. Through the mind thus trained, he was able to pursue his practices with diligence and to listen with care to the teachings of his Guru. This enabled him to take up and follow the subtle hints expressed by the Guru, and to discover the secret of true Self-knowledge in his own being.

> O my mind, I bow to you low.
> From you I have learned a great lesson...
> You did me a compassionate service.
> I will not forget your kindness...
> You discovered the true nature of the Self
> Through pondering on its identity with the Absolute.
> When you finally beheld
> The wondrous nature of my true Self
> All your own fine flights were forgotten.
> Through your grace, Nirbhaya obtained nirvana.
> It was all your own handiwork—
> O my mind, I bow to you low.

Only an enlightened person can truly enjoy life. This is because their heart is free of feelings that lead to frustration and conflict. Swami Nirbhayananda recommends:

> Take up the broom of love and sweep the chamber of your heart,
> Scattering the dust of egoism.

Thus the illumined sages negate the psychological defects that cast a shadow over our understanding and distort our vision. Through right affirmation and practice, we awaken the illumined awareness which replaces the inner darkness. Our heart, purified of selfishness, realizes its essential identity with the Absolute. The world no longer gives rise to fear or ambition, and is accepted as a phenomenal expression, not logically explainable, of that supreme reality. That reality is one with the innermost Self of each and all.

> Enjoy the panorama of the world, but first dissipate the inner darkness.
> You are the lover and the Beloved.

This enlightened understanding is a dominant theme of many of Swami Nirbhayananda's poems. When peace of mind is recommended, it is a means to higher knowledge, enabling us to see more in ourselves and in what we regard as the outer world. The completeness of this capacity for inner vision reveals to the one who possesses it the truth proclaimed in the Upanishads: There is one reality without a second, and that am I. That is the Self of all. In the light of this truth, the world—which before realization seemed all-powerful and real—is exposed as a phenomenal appearance, not a substantial reality. This transformed understanding is indicated in the following lines:

When I could not see, I imagined I saw all,
But with true vision, appearance vanished away.
Without Self-knowledge, none can know rest.

Whether or not this truth is understood, our real Self is always immortal, transcendent and untaintable, and can never be harmed or destroyed by anything. It is the imperishable ground, and both the inner and outer world, with their forms, movement and relationships, are an illusory appearance superimposed on that ground. In so far as the changing world appears within our consciousness, we are at one with it—the support of all appearances. But no appearance whatsoever can interfere with or obscure the purity and transcendence of our true nature as infinite being, consciousness and bliss. This has been called the 'wisdom triumphant' that enables us, if we wish, to enjoy the panorama of the world, while at the same time living in the transcendent universal light of our true nature. It is expressed in the following poem:

All delusion is forgotten. All is bliss.
See the world superimposed phenomenally on Brahman.
Recognize the difference between the substratum and that which is superimposed on it.
Thus has the great Rishi declared!
O darling, see in the Self two powers: activity and rest.

Activity gives rise to the world.
In rest there is neither name nor form.
There is only one consciousness.
My holy Guru has revealed it to me.
Birth and death are caused by activity.
In their absence, there is nothing to give, nothing to take.
I have experienced this state.
It is neither dual nor non-dual.
The mind cannot comprehend it.
O friend, here speech itself becomes silence.

8

THE LIVING HEART OF THE UPANISHADS

> By knowing the self-shining One, all the
> limitations of ignorance end forever. With the
> cessation of all sufferings, there is release from
> birth and death.
>
> *Shvetashvatara Upanishad*, 1:11

THE UPANISHADS are sources of guidance for anyone in
quest of an illumined understanding. Their message
transcends time and place and the boundaries of any
particular religion. They appeal not to our need to
believe, but to our urge to know—the power of enquiry
present in every human mind. And they open a way to
the supreme realization, whereby we know what we
came into the world to know: the ultimate truth about
the nature of experience. We know this truth through
knowing the nature of our true Self.

The living heart of the Upanishads is therefore not
different from the ultimate principle of life and
consciousness within our own being. The Upanishads
teach us about ourselves. The word 'heart' is used as a
metaphor and refers to that place of inner retreat, which
will, when opened up, prove to be without limit, all-
pervading and non-dual.

In one of his writings the sage Shri Shankara relates
the parable of a little boy, a prince, who was discarded
by his parents in infancy and placed in the hands of

foster parents who were poor and used to catch birds in order to make a living. The boy came to feel that he belonged to these folk and was one of them, living in complete ignorance of his princely nature. One day a court official happened to be journeying through the area and, recognizing the boy as the king's son, informed him of his royal descent and awakened him to his true identity.

The parable indicates that our true nature is not the individuality conditioned by the body and the mind, but is the supreme Self that transcends all limitations. Shri Shankara refers to it in the course of his commentary on the verse from the *Brihadaranyaka Upanishad*:

> As a spider moves along the thread which it produces out of itself, and as from a fire tiny sparks fly in all directions, so from the [supreme] Self emanate all organs, all worlds, all gods and all beings. Its secret name is the Truth of truth. The vital force (the life principle) is truth, and It is the Truth of that. (2:1:20)

The teaching is that our true nature, our real Self, is ever at one with the supreme source, as sparks are one with the fire. That source is, as it were, the great Self of all—the Self of the entire universe. It has produced the multiplicity of creatures as a kind of illusory projection or emanation from itself. Therefore we are not separate from the reality and never have been. But like the prince, we have forgotten our true nature, and need to be awakened to it. When this happens, all error falls away, and we know that the essence of our being is one with the supreme.

This information is designed to revive our knowledge of our true nature. It is the main message and purpose of the Upanishads. Their value is to awaken us to our fundamental nature as the infinite consciousness-bliss, and liberate us from the sense that we are anything other than the absolute reality, which is the basis of the world of appearances and of our individual being. It is to arouse in us the knowledge: 'My Self is the Self of all.' Grief and ignorance are cancelled forever. In the words of the *Isha Upanishad*:

> When to the man of realization all beings become the very Self, then what delusion and what sorrow can there be for that seer of oneness? (7)

This Upanishad uses the term oneness, or unity (*ekatvam*) to indicate the awakened understanding. But something deeper than unity is meant, for unity is usually unity of different things, which still remain different things, though bonded together. The realization taught in the Upanishads involves awakening to one's identity with the Self of all *as the only reality.* So to indicate this depth and purity of understanding, another term is used: non-duality, Advaita. Non-duality replaces all differences, including differences between things, between me and what I see, between oneself and ultimate reality.

At the level of sense-experience and mental response, distinctions remain: red is different from green, hot from cold, the song of a robin differs from that of a skylark. But over and above sense-perception and reason, our mind has the potentiality for higher knowledge, for kindling the inner light of wisdom in one's own being. When this special function of the mind is fully awakened, non-duality is realized as the real fact behind the shifting pictures of the world. Our essential identity is revealed as the Self of all. The differences transmitted to the mind through the senses are now seen as appearances which have no reality independent of the limitless power that underlies them.

It is from this standpoint of higher knowledge that differences are transcended in an experience which is by nature infinite bliss and fulfilment. As the *Chandogya Upanishad* expresses it:

> The Infinite is that where one does not see anything else, does not hear anything else, and does not understand anything else... That which indeed is infinite is immortal... It is established in its own glory, or not even in its own glory. (7:24:1)

Far from being a void or a negation of consciousness, this awakened understanding is completeness and fulfilment, indicated by such terms as perfection (*purna*) and bliss (*ananda*).

Returning to this world of differences, which seems real enough until we have realized the true nature of the Self, we can say that the Upanishads form part of the scriptures associated with the Hindu tradition. They are incorporated in that great body of religious instruction called the Vedas. But they mark a break from the Vedic preoccupation with rituals and hymns, that is, with spirituality in its outer forms. Instead, they represent a turning within in order to investigate the true nature of the Self. In this focused internal silence, the seers of the Upanishads experienced a breakthrough in understanding which took them beyond the operations of the intellect, beyond the barriers and unrest of the mental life, and into identification with the ultimate source. They awakened to the fact that our true Self is not different in essence from the supreme power that has manifested out of itself the entire world of appearances.

We remember that the boy prince did not have to become a prince, but he had to be roused out of the condition of ignorance of his princehood. The Upanishads shed light on the fact that we are already complete, fulfilled and self-illumined, but we need to solve this mystery, and by diving deep within, banish ignorance and achieve the same awakened understanding. A verse from the *Katha Upanishad* urges:

Arise, awake, and learn by approaching the excellent ones. The wise ones describe that path to be as impassable as a razor's edge, which when sharpened, is difficult to tread on. (1:3:14)

The Upanishads—and this applies to the higher teachings of any scripture—bring to our attention something that we cannot discover or realize through the ordinary workings of the mind, no matter how clever we are. The mind may come up with many theories, beliefs and speculations, for example, the belief that there must be a God; that we have a soul; that life must have a purpose; that there is a reality behind appearances; that humanity is one family; that the world is dream-like, and may actually be a dream, and so on. These issues are subject to endless debate. But the certainty of truth comes from a power higher than our changing speculations. The means to the experience that satisfies for ever, that cancels all doubts, and from which there is no fall or forgetting, is transmitted through scriptural revelation, mediated by the illumined teachers.

For example, as intelligent enquirers we may be able to determine through reasoning that our fundamental nature is something different and more subtle than the body, senses, mind, intellect, ego, and so on. But when we then ask: 'Well, what am I, if I am not these things?', ordinary experience will not provide the answer. As the *Ashtavakra Gita* tells us:

O Wise One! You may take delight in action or in contemplation, but your mind will still yearn for That which is beyond all objects and in which all desires are extinguished. (16:2)

The ultimate purpose of the Upanishads, transmitted through a Self-realized teacher, is to establish us in that experience 'which is beyond all objects and in which all desires are extinguished'. For the Upanishads tell us clearly, when our mind is freed from confused and biased thinking, 'This Self is the Absolute. It is the All.'

In the Upanishads, the one who wants this knowledge goes to a teacher. He or she asks questions in a spirit of reverence, self-control, love and trust. The teacher gives advice on how to meditate, to think creatively, and live in such a way that we can advance in wisdom, leading to our awakening to Self-knowledge.

As with all great endeavours, there is a certain time in our psychological evolution when we are ready to take up the path to liberation. We are ready when we are sure that no other course of life leads to lasting happiness. As a verse from the *Shvetashvatara Upanishad* (6:20) points out, if we lack the direct experience of the supreme truth, we have as much possibility of ending our sufferings as of rolling up the sky like a piece of leather.

So we need to examine carefully the goals that the world tempts us with, and if we find them mediocre and inadequate, it suggests that we have outgrown such things, and are ready for the higher path. Here is another verse (from the *Mundaka Upanishad*), slightly paraphrased, on this point:

> Having examined these worlds, and finding them all finite and unable to confer lasting fulfilment, one should find a teacher, a knower of the Absolute, make a suitable offering and ask for teachings. (1:2:12)

'Tell me what you know', the pupil is asked, 'and I will tell you what is beyond it.'

If our intuitive feeling is that there is something more to life, something that we really want; if we have a sense of the infinite and the universal, we will find light, insight and delight from absorbing our mind in what the Upanishads tell us about the nature of reality.

As well as metaphysical teachings, we find in the Upanishads profound instructions about spiritual practice. Generally, the method involves turning within ourselves, and seeking for truth in the serenity of our soul. How to make ourselves serene? Meditation is one way. Meditation seems at first to be a narrowing down of our experience from the width, variety and thrill of the outer life, to a kind of internal darkness. But in that apparent darkness is revealed the supreme light, and in that narrowing of our attention is discovered what the

Upanishads call 'the space within the heart'. In this context, the human body is called the City of God, or rather, the City of Brahman, the Absolute, because we discover the supreme reality in our own being.

Let us look at a teaching that makes use of concentration on the heart centre, with the ultimate aim of leading us beyond body-consciousness. It comes in the *Chandogya Upanishad*:

> Within this City of Brahman (the body) there is this small lotus-like dwelling (the 'lotus of the heart', the heart centre). Within it is a small space. That which exists in that space is to be known. That indeed has to be enquired into for realization.

> Should they ask what is it that exists in this small space within the heart, the reply is: 'The space within the heart is as vast as this space that is outside. Within it indeed are included both heaven and earth, as also both fire and air, both sun and moon, lightning and stars. Whatever one has, and whatever one lacks, is included here—in the space within the heart.

> (8:1:1-2)

It is in this hidden, most interior and apparently insignificant dimension of our being that we shall discover the universal wisdom and know ourselves to be the All.

Meditation and withdrawal are procedures we follow in order to bring our mind into attunement with the transcendental truth. Equally important, we should allow the teachings to sink in, so that we remember them and find ourselves brooding about them voluntarily and with deep interest. In the Upanishads, we find that sometimes the student of higher wisdom is sent away in order to take time to think over what has been taught. Then, if further light is sought, the student returns to the teacher and asks in the right spirit for more instructions, as one who is blind seeks sight. For this immutable wisdom is, so to say, the voice of our deeper Self, urging our mind to arise and awake. So we listen with an open mind and afterwards reflect on what we have absorbed in inner quiescence.

We need also to guard against immediately diluting our reception of truth by allowing some distraction or conversation to sweep aside the memory of the teachings. Look on the doctrine of the higher Self, and the way to its realization, as vital information that will fulfil our deepest need.

In the *Chandogya Upanishad*, a pupil comes to a teacher and says:

My knowledge is only intellectual knowledge, and I still experience suffering. I have heard that a knower of Self goes beyond sorrow. I am full of sorrow. O venerable Sir, take me beyond sorrow. (7:1:3)

We are given teachings, and told to make them the focus for reflection and meditation. Then our mind will gain light from the depths of our own being.

Always the idea is that these indications of our higher nature will open a way within us and lead us ultimately to the realization of non-duality through Self-knowledge. This is another distinctive feature of the philosophy of the Upanishads: it is meant to have a fruit, a result. Otherwise, it has no value. There is no interest in speculation as an engaging intellectual activity in itself. As long as our consciousness is subject to apparent limitations, we are in bondage. The way to freedom is to discover what lies at the centre of our own being. 'This Self has to be enquired into for realization.'

The Upanishads form the basis of a practical philosophy. They address the great questions, but resolve these through prompting an inner awakening, and not by prescribing an intellectual point of view. In this way their promise of absolute freedom can be verified in our own direct experience, if the way of life they prescribe is followed. They teach reverence for the supreme power, called Brahman, the Absolute, and stimulate a desire for union with it, and suggest the practical means to effect this union.

In the text called the *Brahma Sutras*, there is the statement:

> The Upanishads acknowledge Brahman (the Absolute) as the Self, and cause it to be known as such. (4:1:3)

But they can only 'cause' our spiritual awakening if we do our part, just as the sun will only cause a fruit tree to grow and flourish if we look after the tree, keep it suitably nourished and protected. But once the fruit—which is Self-realization—has been actualised, the Upanishads have served their purpose.

Implicit in the upanishadic teaching is their own self-effacement in the higher experience of non-duality. 'Know the Self and give up all vain talk.' There is no exaltation of 'the Word', that is, the scriptural Word, for its own sake. For the progression is from the indirect knowledge that we first grasp and assimilate through the words of the scripture, to direct experience of reality: from *Shruti* to *Anubhuti*.

When a spacecraft is to be propelled into space, it needs a powerful launch vehicle to set it on its way. But once the necessary velocity is reached, it can be freed from contact with the launch vehicle. The launch vehicle has served its purpose and falls away. In a similar way, the scriptures are essential to lead us to a realization of the highest truth. But once that realization has come, the scriptures have served their purpose. The direct knowledge of truth, *anubhuti*, is independent of scriptural support. This point—that the scriptures are first necessary and later transcended—is something that each of us is destined to prove in our own experience.

We find a similar teaching given by the Sufi master, Jalaluddin Rumi:

> The Religious Law is like a candle showing the way. Unless you gain possession of the candle, there is no wayfaring; and when you have come on to the way, your wayfaring is the Path; and when you have reached the journey's end, that is the Truth...

> Or the Law may be compared to learning the science of medicine, and the Path to regulating one's diet and taking remedies, and the Truth to gaining health ever-lasting and becoming independent of them both... For it is unseemly to demand a guide after arrival at the goal, and blameworthy to discard the guide before arrival at the goal.
>
> (*Mathnawi*, Preface to Book V)

This higher knowledge is unique because it reveals a dimension of our own being, our 'living heart', so to say, that turns out to be the absolute consciousness beyond relativity and duality. The Upanishads tell us that one who has realized ultimate truth becomes that truth, becomes the reality behind appearances, becomes Brahman, the Absolute.

> Anyone who knows Brahman becomes Brahman.
> (*Mundaka Upanishad*, 3:2:9)

It is not literally a becoming, in the sense of a change in our essential nature. Our essential nature has ever been Brahman. The becoming means the realization of our essential identity as Brahman, the direct experience: 'I am That'. This is the only way the supreme truth can be known; not as an object, not as something else, but through awakening to the fact of our eternal identity with it.

Our true Self is never anything other than the Absolute, the Whole, the All. But, like the boy prince in the story, there seems to be an ignorance, rooted in our mind and sense of individuality, that hides our eternal spiritual sovereignty. This apparent veiling does not change the fact that the Absolute is the true 'I' and is realizable as such to those who follow the upanishadic discipline. As the *Brihadaranyaka Upanishad* assures us:

> And, to this day, whoever knows it as 'I am Brahman' becomes all this universe. (1:4:10)

The meaning is the realization that one is never anything different from the pure, absolute being and consciousness in which the universe appears as a mirage in the desert. This is the way to end the limitations of ignorance and have the everlasting peace and fulfilment that is the normal and unalterable nature of our true Self.

Here are two verses from the *Ashtavakra Gita,* which are based on the wisdom of the Upanishads:

Why should one who knows his Self to be That in which universes rise and fall like waves in the sea, run hither and thither like a suffering creature? (3:3)

Have faith, O Darling, be not deluded! Thou art the Lord of the Universe; thou art Knowledge itself; thou transcendest Nature; verily thou art the Self. (15:8)

9

THE WAY OF CHUANG TZU

THE AIM of Taoism, as of Adhyatma Yoga, is to awaken us to the reality of our true being, which transcends our individuality and is infinite. The word 'sage' is reverentially applied to one who is thus awakened. In the context of the path to Self-knowledge, a sage is one whose psychological limitations have been dissolved in the light of the supreme realization, and what remains is the consciousness of infinity.

Every human being is destined to be a sage. The seeds of enlightenment are at the core of our nature. But these seeds will only germinate if the mind is cultivated in order to bring to life our latent capacity for the 'great understanding'. Otherwise, our thoughts and feelings will range in limited circles, creating restriction and tension, confusion and ultimately despair.

Chuang Tzu was one of the supreme masters of Taoism. Many of his illustrations and comments hint at the possibility of a radical transformation of our human understanding. This is sometimes expressed in terms of moving beyond what is small and confined, into something great and boundless, as when he tells us of a frog living in a well, who has no idea of any universe outside its limits. Viewing the tiny creatures who also live in that habitat, namely, the little crabs, insects and larvae, the frog feels immensely superior and thinks:

'Not one of them compares with me.' One day a great water turtle from the Eastern Sea happens to pass. The frog invites him in to share the comforts and amenities of the well, and enjoy the splendid view. Not only does the turtle get stuck as he tries to get in; he tells the frog about the vast and boundless waters of the ocean and the infinite delights of swimming in it. Hearing this, the frog is bemused and dumbfounded.

There is also the story of the Yellow River, which gets over-excited during the autumn rains when its water level rises above its banks and floods the surrounding fields. At this increase, the river becomes proud, and thinks itself lord of the entire waterlogged landscape. But the great god of the ocean, observing the river's exuberance, leads it onwards to the land's edge. There the river is confronted by waters so boundless that they make its own flow seem a mere trickle. Once more, the small is introduced to the great, and is discomfited.

Still exploring this theme, Chuang Tzu puts aside all analogies and speaks directly about small under-standing and great understanding.*

* Quotations from Chuang Tzu's writings are drawn from *Chuang Tzu – Basic Writings,* trans. Burton Watson, Columbia University Press, New York, 1964; *Chuang Tzu – The Inner Chapters,* trans. A C Graham, Unwin Paperbacks, London, 1986. Reproduced with permission of the publishers. The quotations in poetical form on pages 121 and 123-124 are from *The Way of Chuang Tzu,* Thomas Merton, Unwin Books, London, 1975.

Great understanding is broad and unhurried.
Little understanding is cramped and busy.
Great words are clear and limpid.
Little words are shrill and quarrelsome.
During their waking hours, the bodies of men hustle about anxiously.
With everything they meet, they become entangled.
Day after day, they use their minds in strife, sometimes grandiose, sometimes sly, sometimes petty.
Their little fears are mean and trembly.
Their great fears are stunned and overwhelming.
They bound off like an arrow or a crossbow pellet, certain that they are the arbiters of right and wrong.
They cling to their position as though they had sworn before the gods, sure that they are holding on to victory.
They fade, like fall and winter.
Such is the way they dwindle day by day.
They drown in what they do: you cannot make them turn back.
And when their minds draw near to death, nothing can restore them to the light.

This is a picture of a human life-cycle which Taoism, as well as Adhyatma Yoga, helps us to transcend.

In these words about small understanding, Chuang Tzu describes a way of life and thought that characterizes man when he becomes self-important, apparently master of his surroundings and confidently self-assertive. But he also shows that the whole process is accompanied by fear and anxiety. In this way, human minds become more and more rigid, and averse to any form of inner change. This narrowing of consciousness is contrasted with the expansion and freedom that we enjoy when our self-importance and self-assertion are forgotten, when we cultivate the higher understanding.

In an extension of this same teaching, Chuang Tzu speaks of the Way of Man and the Way of Heaven. If we choose, we can remain simply human, spending our short time on earth trying to satisfy our natural desires and making the best of life. Or we can learn to transcend these limits and take our stand on our true Self, realizing our intrinsic identity with the supreme reality. We then become 'true', enlightened, one who follows the way of Heaven. We are at peace in all circumstances, fearless, free from egoism, and spontaneously going along with what is right for things.

The primary text of Taoism, the *Tao Te Ching*, attributed to Lao Tzu, starts with the lines:

> The Tao that can be told is not the eternal Tao.
> The name that can be named is not the eternal name.
> The nameless is the beginning of heaven and earth...

The word Tao has different levels of meaning according to context. It is usually translated as 'Way'. Ultimately, Tao is nothing less than the Absolute, the supreme reality, which in the Indian tradition is called 'Brahman'. In this sense, the Tao, like Brahman, is that nameless principle which is the ultimate non-dual

117

reality transcending all appearances and limitations. Thus the Tao is the One-without-a-second, the inexpressible Brahman.

Within this ultimate meaning, there are other levels of meaning which are more approachable to human understanding. Tao is identified as the divine source and support of all. This view accepts a world of appearances and the Tao serves as the hidden support of all that appears to exist. This is a clear parallel with the teachings of Adhyatma Yoga. The *Brihadaranyaka Upanishad* declares:

> At the mighty command of that Immutable, the sun, moon, heaven and earth, are held in their positions. At the mighty command of that Immutable, day follows night, the seasons and the years go forward, and the rivers run their courses. (3:8:9)

Chuang Tzu writes, poetically:

> Heaven turns circles, yes!
> Earth sits firm, yes!
> Sun and moon vie for a place, yes!
> Whose is the bow that shoots them?
> Whose is the net that holds them?
> Who is it sits with nothing to do and gives
> them the push that sends them?

Such is Tao.

We also find in the writings of Chuang Tzu such expressions as 'When Tao was lost' or 'When Tao went into decline'. Here, we may suggest that Tao means something more like insight, spiritual wisdom, an enlightened understanding, something that can be cultivated or ignored by human beings. So when it is said: 'Tao is in decline' or 'is lost', it means that our capacity for spiritual vision has been temporarily eclipsed and people tend to live their lives in the realm of 'small understanding', based largely on selfish considerations, insisting on the validity of their own restricted vision, and seeing nothing beyond, like the frog in the well.

A further meaning of Tao is that it is the source of inspiration in human affairs. If we harmonize ourselves with the way of heaven, our actions become unselfish and inspired. This inspiration—this form of Tao—is available in any walk of life, as long as one is sufficiently dedicated to the task in hand. Such inspiration is natural to us, as long as we take refuge in our deeper centre, effacing the sense of narrow egoism through absorption in the work.

Far from being an elite way of life, Chuang Tzu shows how this inspiration of Tao can infuse any activity. The cook, Ting, for example, was congratulated by his master for his brilliant method of preparing food. Hearing this, Ting turned to his master and said: 'Method? What I follow is Tao, beyond all methods.' Then he explained how his long experience had led him to a kind of self-forgetting concentration, enabling his work to proceed smoothly without interference. This he called 'following Tao'.

Finally, Tao can also mean the theory and practice of the way to enlightenment. The student of Tao is expected to put the teachings into practice, and so can be said to be 'practising Tao', much in the way that one adopts the values and carries out the practices that are prescribed in the Yoga of Self-knowledge.

These various meanings attached to the word Tao are expounded and illustrated in *The Book of Chuang Tzu*. Its 33 chapters are filled with stories, dialogues and philosophical reflections. Chuang Tzu is nowadays considered to be the author of the first seven chapters, called for this reason the 'Inner Chapters', while the rest of the text is an extension of his way of thought and expression, and probably includes further fragments composed by him.

In one of the dialogues, Chuang Tzu is asked: 'This thing called Tao—where is it to be found?' Chuang Tzu, who often appears as a character in his own book, answers: 'There is nowhere it is not to be found.' Then his questioner, Tung-kuo, says: 'But you must be more specific.' Chuang Tzu answers: 'It is in the ant.' 'As low a thing as that?' 'It is in the weeds.' 'As low as that?' 'It is in the waste of the body.' Tung-kuo had nothing more to say. Then Chuang Tzu said: 'None of your questions is to the point. You must not expect to find the way in any particular place. There is no thing that escapes its presence.'

Then the sage teaches, in effect, that it is not by looking through one's physical eyes at this or that object that one can expect to see the Tao. What is needed, he says, is 'tranquil quietude, hushed purity, harmony and repose. Then knowledge itself will spring up in you, and this knowledge has no limit.' This echoes a meditation text used in Adhyatma Yoga:

OM

WISDOM ARISES FROM THE DEPTH OF OUR BEING,
WHEN, IN THE STILLNESS AND PURITY OF THE
HEART, THE FINITE MEETS THE INFINITE.

OM

Tao, when fully realized, turns out to be our true source and home, identified in Yoga as our innermost Self or Consciousness. Chuang Tzu represents this in the following lines:

Fishes are born in water. Man is born in Tao.
If fishes, born in water, seek the deep shadow of pond and pool,
All their needs are satisfied.
If man, born in Tao, sinks into the deep shadow of non-action,
To forget aggression and concern,
He lacks nothing, his life is secure.
All the fish needs is to get lost in water.
All man needs is to get lost in Tao.

How can this universal principle called Tao be awakened in ordinary life? Here we return to the ancient ideal of the sage—the Self-realized human being. This ideal is also at the heart of the upanishadic wisdom. As the *Brihadaranyaka Upanishad* says: 'Knowing It alone, one becomes a sage.' (4:4:22) The word 'It' denotes Brahman, or Tao. The sage has re-discovered the ultimate source of being, the true Self. This is why Chuang Tzu calls the sage one who is 'true'. Sagehood is the completion and fulfilment of human development.

Every human being is a sage in the making. The potentiality for enlightenment is latent in everyone, for Tao is the divine essence within all human beings. The sage is one who has broken the magic spell that holds the mind in thrall to appearances, and has sought out and realized his own essential nature.

We may note a contrast between the ideal of the sage and that of the saint. Saints are usually associated with a particular religion, and have earned their saint-hood, in the eyes of posterity, through holy living based on faith, devotion and self-sacrifice.

The life of the sage may be equally holy, yet another dimension is emphasized: that of knowledge. Always, with the sage, the key thing is not so much: 'What has been done?' but 'What has been known, realized, understood through and through?' The sage has a particular kind of knowledge. This is not the know-ledge gained from a book, but direct experience of spiritual reality. It is the same knowledge spoken of in the Upanishads as the basis of all knowledge, knowing which nothing remains to be known, and knowing which one's thirst to know is satisfied for ever.

Those familiar with Chinese history will know that at the time of Chuang Tzu, another ideal of sagehood was being taught in China. This was based on the teachings of Confucius, who promulgated righteous conduct and behaviour, inspired by feelings of warmth and human-heartedness towards one's fellow men. The teachings of Confucius are an application of the principle known as 'dharma', the law of righteousness.

For Chuang Tzu this ideal is not the goal of human existence. It is not enough in order to bring about that final understanding which enables one to realize one's essential unity with the infinite and blissful Tao. Chuang Tzu's writings sometimes humorously show Confucius sitting at the feet of the Taoist masters in order to learn true wisdom.

Here is a short description of a sage by Chuang Tzu, which shows how his ideal of sagehood both embraces and transcends that of Confucius.

The man in whom Tao acts without impediment
Harms no other being by his actions,
Yet he does not know himself to be 'kind',
to be 'gentle'.
The man in whom Tao shines in its full glory
Does not bother with his own interests,

And does not despise others who do.
He does not struggle to make money,
And does not make a virtue of poverty.
He goes his way without relying on others,
And does not pride himself on walking alone.
While he does not follow the crowd,
He won't complain of those who do.
Rank and reward make no appeal to him,
Disgrace and shame do not deter him.
He is not always looking for right and wrong,
Always deciding 'yes' or 'no'.
The ancients said, therefore,
'The man of Tao remains unknown.
Perfect virtue produces nothing.
'No-Self' is 'True-Self.'
And the greatest man
Is nobody.

This range of values differs from our normal way of thinking, where we tend to place more weight on outer signs than on inner essentials. The contrast is illustrated in another story that is found in *The Book of Chuang Tzu*.

A certain sage lived in a tiny house. It was hardly more than four walls. The roof was thatched but broken in many places, so that the floor was damp. One day a grand acquaintance came to call on the sage. There he was, singing and playing his lute. The grand person approached in his carriage, but it was too wide to come up the lane. He was dressed in a fine robe of royal blue. The sage, dressed in a hemp robe and with heel-less slippers, went to the gate to welcome his visitor. The visitor said: 'Goodness, what distress you are in, sir.'

The sage replied: 'I have heard that if one lacks wealth, that is called poverty. If one studies Tao, but cannot put it into practice, that is called distress. I am poor, it is true, but I am not in distress.'

How does the sage reach this position of repose and independence? If every man and woman is a potential sage, how do we bring out this potentiality, so that the transcendent in us, the Tao, may express itself without impediment? 'Impediment' is a revealing word. It comes from a Latin word which means 'baggage': impedimenta. For Tao to work through us without impediment, we ourselves must be prepared to open our hands and let the baggage we are carrying slip away. What this letting go means in practice is illustrated in the story called Keng's Disciple.

A man approached the teacher, Keng-sang, com-plaining that he was unable to put his teachings into practice. All this instruction about inner stillness and reducing one's thoughts, made no sense to him. Keng, after a brief interview, decided that he himself lacked the talent to transform this pupil, and said: 'Why don't you go south and visit Lao Tzu?'

After a seven days' journey, the man, Nan-jung Chu, approached the hermitage of Lao Tzu. Lao Tzu saw him coming and asked: 'Has Keng sent you here?'

'Yes sir'. 'Then', said Lao Tzu, 'who are all those people you've brought with you?'

The pupil spun round in astonishment to look. There was nobody there. 'Don't you know what I mean?' asked Lao Tzu. The crowd of people refers to the conventional concepts of right and wrong, good and bad, life and death, hope and fear which we carry with us everywhere. These deep-rooted convictions form, so to say, a thick covering over our true being, so that the light within us cannot be released. The teachings we hear cannot penetrate deeply. We have ears, yet do not hear.

In terms of Chuang Tzu's image, this inner throng of fixed ideas and instinctive reactions needs to be thinned and finally dispersed. This is the first real challenge for any aspirant to higher knowledge, and it is ongoing.

The pupil then tells Lao Tzu about the distress and confusion he feels. It is a negative self-assessment, yet, looked at in a wider perspective, this man has taken a step forward in his inner evolution. He has become dissatisfied with his state. He knows something is wrong with his understanding, and that the solution must be an introvertive one, involving sorting out his own mind.

Here is someone unlike the well-frog. The frog was self-satisfied and not interested in investigating whether there was anything beyond the well. But this man intuitively feels the need to expand his consciousness, and that there must be a more desirable state of being available to him. So he asks Lao Tzu to be allowed to stay, and then spends the next ten days in solitude, trying to resolve his psychological difficulties by cultivating good qualities and getting rid of faults. When he emerges from this course, Lao Tzu notices his 'scrubbed and shining' look, but discerns that there is still something smouldering within. 'There are still bad things there.' He then gives some teachings to lift the mind above personal considerations, and hints that it is not by endless thinking that one gains relief, but by self-forgetfulness in inner stillness.

The episode sheds light on the way of 'great understanding'. Unlike psychoanalysis and other therapies that focus on our personal make-up and our past, the spiritual meditations help us to quieten the whole of the mind, and to forget its present and past contents—at least, for the time being. Our personal history is irrelevant to the deeper experience we are now seeking.

Chuang Tzu rarely gives methods of meditation, but it is clear that one of his main practices is emptying the mind: the ability to say 'Not wanted, not wanted' to the thoughts and mind-pictures as they arise. In the *Tao Te Ching* it is said:

I do my utmost to attain emptiness.
I hold firmly to stillness.
...Returning to one's roots is known as stillness.

The liberating way is to forget ourselves, and by subjective withdrawal, to go beyond the talkative level of the mind, into the still, illuminated depth of our eternal being. 'In quality of mind, it is depth that matters.' (*Tao Te Ching*)

Chuang Tzu comes to the heart of the teachings of Adhyatma Yoga in his story of the old woman of clear complexion. It is an illustration of the subtle process known in Yoga as spiritual discrimination. This involves an acute self-examination to uncover the innermost principle of eternal reality, unchanging selfhood. It is done through setting aside those transient aspects of experience that our self seems to be identified with. This is not a physical process but an inner one of sharpening our faculty of self-analysis.

A certain elderly woman was asked: 'You are old in years and yet your complexion is that of a child. Why is this?' She replied: 'I have heard the Way'. She is asked: 'Can the Way be learnt?' And she answers, in effect, that the Way cannot be learnt in the way learning is usually understood—that is, by accumulating information. It is more a matter of unlearning—of disidentifying oneself from all that is limited and finite in experience.

The woman explains how she tried to transmit her mystical knowledge to a certain Pu-liang Yi. She said that after teaching him for three days, he was able to put the world outside himself. Then, she said: 'I kept at him for seven more days, and after that he was able to put things outside himself.' After further instruction, he was able to put life outside himself. Thus able to make this deep inner discrimination, separating his inmost consciousness from body and mind, he gained some degree of inner light.

> After he had put life outside himself, he was able to achieve the brightness of dawn, and when he had achieved the brightness of dawn, he could see his own aloneness. After he had managed to see his own aloneness, he could do away with past and present, and after he had done away with past and present, he was able to enter where there is no life and no death.

In this story, there is a transmission of teachings from the woman who had 'heard' the Way to the man, Pu-liang Yi, whose mind was also able to 'hear' properly the words of truth and put them into practice. He is taught, in inner stillness, how to separate his essential identity from the outer coverings of worldly thoughts and body-consciousness. Through this un-learning, this negating, he is able to realize his true nature as immortal and infinite. This is a precise parallel to the path of Yoga, leading to its higher practice of saying: 'Neti, neti—not this, not this' to all that is changing, limited and not the innermost Self.

Chuang Tzu's vision is rooted in transcendence, while his practical teachings demonstrate how the influence of Tao well-lived will naturally produce harmony in society, once we have overcome our narrow way of looking at things. This path to deeper insight involves seeing beyond appearances and being prepared courageously to drop conventional values, in favour of a wider and more loving vision.

A certain Taoist teacher, he relates, had a group that included both the Prime Minister and a man who had incurred the punishment of having one of his feet cut off for a crime committed earlier in his life. The Prime Minister said to this disciple: 'Now if I go out first, then I want you to stay behind. And if you go out first, I'll stay behind.' It was clear that the Prime Minister did not want to be seen in the company of an ex-criminal.

The next day, they were sitting together on the same mat before the Master. When the lesson ended, the Prime Minister again made his request, announcing that he would leave first, and insisting quite firmly that the other fellow should remember that he was Prime Minister, and should stay behind for a while, as requested.

This disciple, whose name was Shen-t'u Chia, then said: 'Within the gates of our Master, is there such a thing as a Prime Minister? You take delight in being a Prime Minister and pushing people behind you. But I have heard that if the heart's mirror is bright, no dust settles on it. If it is not bright, dust settles. When we keep company with a holy man long enough, no crime remains in us. You regard our Master as a great man, and yet you talk like this?'

At this, the Prime Minister replied: 'I think you ought to look to your own virtues, or, to judge from your appearance, your lack of them!'

Then Shen-t'u Chia said: 'Many commit wrong-doings and are able to conceal them very cleverly, and thus escape what happened to me. However, I accept what has happened and make no attempt to conceal it. But let me tell you this. I have been going around with the Master for nineteen years now, and was never aware that I'm a man with one foot. Now you and I are supposed to be wandering outside the realm of forms and bodies, and yet you insist on judging me by my appearance. Don't you think that's a crime?' At this, the Prime Minister looked uncomfortable, and begged Shen-t'u Chia to say no more.

Although the Prime Minister comes out badly in this story, it would be wrong to judge him too harshly. Every human mind has its prejudices, which influence the way we look at people. Still, as his fellow disciple pointed out, both were walking a path which would lead beyond all prejudice and duality. The Prime Minister was fortunate to have this inner obstacle brought to his attention, for he could now work on himself in order to transcend it.

This last story comes from the inner chapter called The Sign of Virtue Complete. Here, once again, Chuang Tzu shows how our habitual ideas and judge-ments form a blindfold preventing us from seeing with the inner eye of wisdom, and from enjoying true rest and fearlessness.

'If the heart's mirror is bright, no dust will settle; but if it is not bright, dust settles.' In Taoism, as in Yoga, the wonderful potentialities for this deeper knowledge are present in everyone. But to realize the bliss and infinity of our true nature, we have to pay attention to the heart's mirror, and do our best to live according to the spiritual values. Then, in the resulting peace and purity, a new way of knowing will dawn, bringing completeness and fulfilment.

Like Brahman, the ultimate nature of the Tao is transcendent, free from attributes, the All. Chuang Tzu indicates this when he writes:

> The Way has its reality and its signs, but is without action or form... It is its own source, its own root... It exists beyond the highest point, and yet you cannot call it high; it exists beneath the limit of the six directions, and yet you cannot call it deep. It was born before heaven and earth, and yet you cannot say it has been there for long...

This ever pure and perfect reality is one without a second, and is our innermost Self.

10

TEACHINGS OF THE SAGE ASHTAVAKRA

THE ASHTAVAKRA GITA is a short classical text, composed in the Sanskrit language, which gives the highest teachings of the Yoga of Self-Knowledge. Like the *Bhagavad Gita*, it is in verse, and its title means 'the song of (the sage) Ashtavakra'. This *Gita* is not so much a book of systematic instruction as an attempt to indicate through words the inexpressible nature of enlightenment. One of its chapters begins with a verse of salutation to the supreme reality:

> Salutations to That which is bliss, peace and light, with the dawning of the knowledge of which, all delusion as to the phenomenal universe passes away like a dream. (18:1)

This realization is the goal of life, and such verses help to make us conscious of that goal.

The text initially takes the form of a discourse between the teacher, Ashtavakra, and a pupil, King Janaka. Both these figures are well-known in the literature of ancient India. Janaka's position as a ruler living an active life in the world is significant. It denotes that the teaching is available to all serious seekers, whether they work in society or live in solitude as contemplatives.

Janaka had learnt that there is a higher knowledge that gives, not information, but lasting fulfilment through direct experience of the reality underlying the universe, and he thirsts for this experience. It differs from intellectual knowledge, and is essentially something that transcends words and the grasp of thought. The transformative power of this higher knowledge is indicated in the verse:

Knowledge of the imperishable Essence makes a worldly, active and eloquent man inactive, silent and wise. (15:3)

Nonetheless, in the tradition of Adhyatma Yoga, teachings are expressed through words and ideas. For the thoughts of those who are enlightened have a quality which sets them apart from intellectual concepts and appeals to a deeper level of our being. If such statements are received and applied to our practice, they guide our mind to a higher state of consciousness.

Though the *Ashtavakra Gita* is presented as an interchange between teacher and pupil, Janaka asks just three questions throughout the whole text, and these questions are put in the opening verse.

O Lord, tell me this: how does a man acquire knowledge of Truth, and how liberation, and how the practice of renunciation? (1:1)

He receives an answer from Ashtavakra which takes up the rest of the first chapter. When we meet Janaka again, at the start of the second chapter, he speaks, but he no longer asks questions. He appears as one who has realized the inner meaning of the teachings he is given, and now he too expresses himself as an enlightened sage.

> How wonderful! I am tranquil, taintless, pure knowledge transcending matter. Until now I have been deceived by illusion. (2:1)

Janaka's last question: 'How does man acquire the practice of renunciation?' reminds us that there is a sacrifice to be made for this knowledge, a price that is not easily paid. As a king, he was rich and could buy anything he wished. But the liberating knowledge is not for sale. One may purchase books which contain words of wisdom, but one cannot buy the higher and trans-cendental meaning that inspired the authors of these books. Janaka realized that in order to experience ultimate truth, something had to be renounced.

In the society of the time, there were many renunciates—wandering monks and ascetics, who had apparently given up everything. At first sight, then, the meaning of renunciation, and what you had to renounce, seems obvious. There are even formal rules for living such a life. Janaka had the insight to know that there is a deeper renunciation, which is not the same as physical renunciation. But what does this entail?

Tradition relates how Janaka first offered half his kingdom to Ashtavakra, but the sage said: 'Why do you call this kingdom yours? Who ruled it before you, and who before him? You have not created it, you cannot control it.' The king then offered his body in service. This too was refused with the words: 'But is the body yours? Did you create it? Can you protect it from disease and old age?'

This prompted Janaka to pause and reflect, and consider what actually did belong to him, if anything. Finally, he said: 'My Lord, I know that you have enlightened me considerably. I offer my mind to you.' At this, Ashtavakra was pleased. 'That is right, my son. Henceforth, do not think a single thought for yourself, for your body or for your kingdom. You have given me your mind, it is no longer yours.' Janaka realized that the mind, with its fixed ideas, habitual patterns of thought and self-will, was the real barrier to self-understanding, and he recognized the wisdom of letting go of his sense of identity with the mind, through offering it to the highest spiritual wisdom represented by the sage.

What does this mean in practice? True renunciation is based on our willingness to revise our conviction of 'self' in the light of the teachings on Self-knowledge. Self is the ultimate light of consciousness which reveals the body and mind, and in a certain sense, is the permanent, unchanging 'subject' under whose light all else is experienced as transient events, radically different from the 'knowing' Self, and therefore not the Self. Hence a verse declares:

> My nature is Knowledge and nothing other than Knowledge. Verily the universe is revealed under the light of my Self. (2:8)

This all-illumining awareness of the immutable Self is sometimes referred to as 'intelligence', but the context shows that the pure, transcendent consciousness of the Self is meant, not the limited intelligence of the mind:

> If, detaching thyself from thy sense of identity with the body, thou remain at rest in Intelligence, thine will be spontaneous bliss, eternal peace and liberation from the imagined bondage. (1:4)

To develop this detachment, or renunciation, is to lift our sense of identity from the limited personality to the true Self. For renunciation in the highest sense is disidentification. It has much to do with renouncing false views and ideas of selfhood, and with taking to heart the view that one's own nature is the divine Self which is Pure Consciousness, and nothing else.

Before going more deeply into the meaning of true identification, Ashtavakra speaks of the state of mind that aids our progress in wisdom:

O Friend, if thy aim in life is liberation, then shun sense objects as poison and pursue as nectar, forgiveness, simplicity of life, compassion, contentment and truth. (I:2)

Anyone who is sympathetic to spiritual teachings of any tradition, can warm to the virtues mentioned in the second half of this verse: forgiveness, simplicity of life, compassion, contentment and truth. Such virtues are socially friendly and embracing, and people who live in this way are likely to be good companions. But the one who benefits most from this unifying and positive attitude is the one who practises it. In Yoga it is taught that such mental tendencies have a purifying and tranquillizing effect on our own minds, hence they are highly desirable, like nectar.

The first half of the verse seems to be a more difficult proposition. To urge us to 'shun sense objects as poison' is a strong statement and needs some qualification. It is clear that if we literally shunned sense objects, then, at best, our life would become like one of house-arrest, or at worst, it would be an anaesthetised existence that could not last very long. Sense objects take in the whole realm of outer experience, from food to books, from work to learning, music, play, sport, exercise—everything. So what does it mean, and how can such an injunction help us, who are plunged in an ocean of sense objects and experiences which form the very setting of our life?

The first point to note is that Ashtavakra said: 'If your goal is liberation'. Liberation is the highest goal of life, and the ultimate end of all our strivings. But it is not the only goal recognized in the *Sanatana Dharma* (the 'eternal religion'). Other acknowledged aims include sense-enjoyment, wealth, learning, philanthropy, and the accumulation of religious merit. These are natural pursuits at certain stages of our development. But sooner or later, we realize that nothing achieved in these areas brings lasting happiness. Desires tend to lead to more desires, and when unfulfilled, breed anger and frustration.

After innumerable experiences in this restless sea of gaining and losing, the mind becomes more keenly aware of the passing and changing nature of human happiness. It is then that the goal of liberation, with its promise of eternal joy that transcends the world, makes its appeal. This growing understanding includes a clear perception of the transient and dreamlike nature of all our experiences in the world, whether pleasing or painful.

> One who has finally learnt that it is in the nature of objects to come into existence, to change and finally to pass away, he easily finds rest through detachment and is freed from suffering. (11:1)

The quality of detachment becomes a natural attitude once we have recognized the transient nature of

experience and the elusive character of joy and fulfilment. Liberation is ultimate joy and fulfilment, and it
is also natural detachment, because it means the
realization of the pure, transcendent and infinite nature
of the true Self, not conditioned by anything. So in this
sense, over-emphasis of our bond with anything finite
and limited is bound to distort our understanding of
what we really are, and keep us confined within the
world of limitations. Detachment means to value life's
gifts, but not to cling to anything as if our happiness
depended on it. Thus equipped, we are able to recover
our calm and balance even when our desires meet with
frustration. For we recognize that the ground of our
being is untouched by vicissitude.

This attitude is partnered with our wish to deepen
our inner enquiry, and not waste time and energy on
that which leaves our mind in a lowered and agitated
state. Daily meditation nurtures the inner strength and
courage to say 'No' to anything that threatens our
spiritual advance.

Having indicated the qualifications, Ashtavakra
proceeds to enlighten Janaka with the highest teaching
—that the true Self is not the body, not the mind, not
the ego, but that principle of pure intelligence, being
and bliss, and is the natural state of the soul. Any other
view of the Self is the result of a misunderstanding—a
wrong identification caused by what is called 'spiritual
ignorance'. Janaka is therefore given clues to the real
Self-knowledge.

It is our ignorance of the true nature of the Self that gives rise to false views about it. But when we learn how to reduce unnecessary and wasteful mental activity, and make the mind still and peaceful, the insight will dawn that there is a deeper dimension of self that transcends the limitations of body, mind, time and space. It is like the falling away of veils, or the dissolving of clouds that hide an inner sun. When the clouds part, the sun shines through, and when we learn to saturate our mind and feelings in the liberating ideas about the deeper Self within, there will be a clearing of some of the long-cherished self-images that prevent us from enjoying the true glory and infinity of our own being.

The path of Yoga is like a step ladder leading upwards, but it does not lead upwards to an unnatural position. It is more like the case of a man who has fallen into a deep pit. The ladder of Yoga is made available to save him from his predicament. He climbs that ladder step by step, escapes from the pit, and finds himself back on level ground. Now he can walk freely, and has no need to carry the ladder about with him.

One's real Self is the source of happiness. Several verses of the *Ashtavakra Gita* end with the words: 'Be happy!' or 'Live in bliss!' For example:

My child, study and discussion of different philosophies will not establish thee in the Self. Forget all, and be happy. (16.1)

The conventional belief is that in order to be happy we must achieve and acquire, and that happiness depends on our possessions and our connections with other people. But to think in this way is to be under a delusion. Unconditioned happiness comes from quietening the mental activity and allowing the deeper aspect of our being to reveal itself.

This natural bliss is present at the centre of our being as its essence. In the Upanishads there is a passage which says that the happiness of a youthful king, commanding all power and pleasure, and even the happiness of the gods, is small compared with the happiness of one who is free from desire. The same point is made again and again in the *Ashtavakra Gita*:

> Anxiety produces misery and nothing else. He who realizes this relinquishes all desires and is calm and happy. (11:5)

> Desire constitutes the only bondage; to be freed from it is liberation. By cultivating indifference to worldly objects, one obtains the bliss of realization. (10:4)

The pure witnessing Intelligence is the only element in experience that remains the same in the past, present and future. This is the real Self, eternal, perfect, complete:

> Let the body last until the end of the world period, or perish today; nothing can be added to or subtracted from thy Self, which is pure Knowledge. (15:10)

One and the same Self underlies all phenomena, and its universality is indicated in several verses of the *Ashtavakra Gita* through the image of an infinite ocean.

I am the limitless ocean in which, on the rising of the wind of the mind, the worlds are produced, as waves on the sea. (2:23)

Such verses signify that the Self is all-pervasive. Just as there are no waves, bubbles or foam without the sea, so too everything in experience is a phenomenal manifestation of the one great reality. Ashtavakra speaks of the rising of the wind of the mind. It is this mental activity that gives rise to our experience of the world. There is also the idea that these waves, churned up by the wind, exist in a medium that, without this wind, is still and waveless. The pivot of the universe of appearances is the human mind. Its state of peace or disturbance completely conditions our experience of the world. This is simply stated in an earlier verse:

He who thinks himself to be free, is free, and he who thinks himself to be bound, is bound. True is the saying, 'as a man thinks, so he becomes.' (1:11)

All our knowledge of the world comes to us through one single organ of experience: our own individualized mind. It is not unreasonable to think that if the mental waves of agitation and desire were allowed to die down, a very different perception of reality would come to light. Another verse takes this teaching a step further:

> In me, the infinite ocean, arises the imagined universe. Tranquil and attributeless, my Self abides for ever. (7:3)

This verse suggests a twofold vision: the calm acceptance of the world appearance within one's own infinite being, and also an underlying tranquillity based on the realization that nothing that appears can alter the immortal transcendent nature of the Self. This great affirmation is made from the point of view of enlightenment. The words 'In me' are not referring to an individual mind. They point to the fully revealed Self, which is compared to an infinite ocean. It is an inner vision that cannot be described in words. But such words equip us with key images and concepts that help us to probe deeper into that same impersonal Self which is our own true being. This verse accepts the rise of appearances in one's own infinite being as a kind of imagination. The true Self remains tranquil and unaffected, and, as the Upanishad declares, 'That Thou Art'.

Tranquillity is the necessary condition of mind in which the higher insights are received. Yoga involves making experiments in tranquillity through meditation, and through a life of purpose, so that the supreme reality can be clearly brought to light in one's own experience. All the practices of Yoga, like self-control and concentration, are means to an end, not ends in themselves. The Yoga practices help to bring the mind to peace, and to sharpen its spiritual awareness. Yoga is not a lifetime's pursuit; it leads to a definite result, a 'fruit'.

> He who is always contented, who is unattached to any object, who ever enjoys solitude, he has obtained the fruit of spiritual knowledge and of the practice of Yoga. (17:1)

But the idea of making efforts towards a goal turns out to be a provisional teaching. From the standpoint of the higher knowledge, the goal of enlightenment is realized as ever-achieved. In the words of Shri Shankara, the Self is 'ever pure, ever free, ever enlightened'. Enlightenment is the nature of the Self. Ashtavakra makes it clear that when the Self is realized, all talk of achievement is not only irrelevant but inappropriate and misleading.

Misunderstandings arise because we are seeking something which, at the deepest level of our being, we already are. No one makes efforts unless they believe that something has not been achieved, and that our exertions will help us to achieve it. Yet this way of thinking, with regard to self-discovery, places our innermost Self at a distance, so to say. It affirms a gap where there is no gap. This subtle paradox is stated thus:

All are afflicted by reason of their exertions. Alas! this is understood by none, but he who is wise achieves emancipation through this very teaching. (16:4)

What happens in the mind of the seeker in this position?

To attempt to think of the Self, which is beyond the range of thought, is only to create a new thought. Abandoning such a thought, I abide in peace. (12:7)

Thought will not produce Self-knowledge. Mental quiescence—inner peace—opens the way. Between these two alternatives, thinking and inner peace, there is a practice of crucial importance in our inner quest: right affirmation. This means affirming our true nature as an established fact, basing our practice on the affirmations given by the holy sages. The stronger, deeper, more faithful and confident our affirmation of our identity with the true Self, the weaker becomes our sense of identity with the not-self. This is called true identification.

The Vedanta teaching is that our infinite consciousness appears to be conditioned and limited by our body and mind through a kind of error or illusion. Right affirmation undermines this illusion, and will eventually revive our certainty of identity with the one reality. Such affirmations are not concerned with thinking of the Self, but with embracing the true Self as our very being here and now. The affirmations help to dissolve individual egoism, re-establishing us in lasting peace and fulfilment. Our true nature is perfect being, and this is affirmed in the following verse: (20:1)

In my perfect being, neither the elements, nor the body, nor the sense organs, nor the thinking principle, nor the void, nor despondency, exist.

11

ENLIGHTENED ACTION—THE EXAMPLE OF CHRIST

WHAT IS THE motive for action? At a basic level, it is to secure what is pleasurable and avoid pain or danger. But motive suggests premeditation, and many of our actions, like shielding our eyes from a sudden glare, appear to spring automatically, without the preparation of thought.

Motive emerges more clearly as our sense of individuality evolves, along with the values we feel are worth pursuing. These may be crude or refined, self-centred or altruistic. But all such motivation assumes our status as an individualized conscious entity whose nature is to formulate desires, act and experience. The 'I' is wedded to its organs of action and knowledge.

Knowledge of ultimate truth dissolves this limitation. It is certain knowledge that the real Self, which is the ultimate light of consciousness and the ground of being, is independent and infinite, never conditioned by the physical and psychological environments, or the desires that normally rule human life. Identification with the infinite 'I' is realization of its non-duality. The sense of 'I' as an individualized ego, the subject and owner of our experience, a centre of unique value and significance, is transcended.

The ego-sense, in fact, is never a durable reality, but a transient and intermittent feature of the ephemeral world of thought. Its apparent genuineness is due to its dependence on a deeper source of consciousness and power—the real Self, which is reflected, as it were, in our mind as our ego-sense, like the sun reflected in water. But a reflection is an appearance, not a reality. Reflections are not only phenomenal; they are conditioned by the limitations of the medium in which they are reflected. Self-realization is self-identification with the source, not its phenomenal reflection in the mind, as ego. The world, the body, the mind with its thoughts and responses may continue to appear within experience, but they have no independent existence; their source and essence, and the cause of their knowability, is one's infinite Self.

For one who knows the highest truth, and who appears to continue to act and to experience with instruments (body and mind) and in an environment (the world) known to be phenomenal, selfish motivation is impossible, because there is no limited self. If the knower of truth is involved in life's complications and relationships, neither desire nor duty dictate the moves, but they are prompted, as it were, by a source that is free from all narrowness and delusion—directives, so to say, from the reality itself, a pure and perfect 'motivation' in harmony with the supreme good. Such workings, expressed by those at one with

149

the 'One-without-a-second', may be called 'enlightened action'.

The life of Jesus exemplifies this highest mode of action—impersonal, transcending egoism, going beyond conventional ideas of goodness, yet intent on the highest good of all. Like all the great teachers of truth, he came to lift humanity to a higher state of consciousness. He lived and preached the supreme wisdom, the way to everlasting joy.

For those who are open to his influence, that transmission of the living light of truth flows through his every word and gesture. This is so even in seemingly casual interchanges.

An example of truth casually imparted comes when Jesus first speaks in the *Gospel of St John*. The place was near the River Jordan, where John had administered the baptism of Christ the day before. The next day John was there with two of his disciples, Andrew and one who is not named.

John the Baptist sees Jesus walking nearby. His attention is absorbed in the sight. He says to the disciples: 'Behold, the lamb of God!' The two disciples are then drawn irresistibly to Jesus, and follow him. Jesus turned, and seeing them following, says just three words: 'What seek ye?' They answer: 'Rabbi, where dwellest thou?' Jesus answers: 'Come and see.' The Bible continues: 'They came and saw... and abode with him that day.' (*John*, 2:35-39)

'What seek ye?' This is the most important question we can put to our own mind as we go about our life. It is not the metaphysical question: 'What am I?' It is not a question about our ultimate aspiration. It is the practical question that always has to be put to our mind to check the state of our inner life here and now. 'What seek ye, O mind?'

Seeking, in this context, means: 'What is the heart pining for? What is the mind gravitating towards—the small or the great?' The most rewarding quest is for the ultimate security of the wisdom of Self-knowledge. 'What seek ye, O mind? This very moment, what seek ye?' For Jesus there is only one worthwhile answer: 'Seek ye first the kingdom of God, and all things shall be added unto thee.' 'Seek and ye shall find.'

In terms of the non-dual teachings, it is to seek with diligence to realize the deeper reality within our own being, our innermost Self, and to know our Self to be the source of peace and joy, and one with the supreme power that underlies and reveals the universe. 'I and my father are one' applies to the Self of all, the universal 'I' which replaces personal egoism.

We may therefore learn to contemplate Christ as a perfect personification of the life of illumined action. To be able to appreciate the infinite wisdom transmitted by Jesus through his teachings and his life, calls for an openness of mind and the re-orientation of the chief desires of our heart—from the pursuit of passing gratifications to the quest for the realization of eternal life in our own being. Then there can be that heart-to-heart transmission of higher experience, which reveals to us that Christ is none other than our own true Self.

In contemplating Jesus's life, we may be reminded of the saying 'the good is the enemy of the best'. It was not wicked people who opposed Jesus, but basically good people—good according to their orthodox understanding. Several, like Nicodemus and Joseph of Arimathea, were ready to welcome his influence as liberating, but the majority, it seems, were rooted in their own ideas of righteousness and closed their minds to his message. This is why Jesus told the Pharisees: 'I do not come to teach the righteous—those who are whole do not need a physician.' (*Matthew* 9:9-13) The 'wholeness' Jesus refers to in this instance is not that of ultimate freedom, but a stage on the way—a stage which has to be transcended if one is to awaken to Self-knowedge.

These limited conventional views about goodness, religious observance and correct behaviour were shared to some extent even by his close disciples. When little children were brought into his proximity, the disciples sought to ward them off, perhaps imagining they would create disorder and waste the time of the master, diverting him from his important work of teaching and healing. But Jesus rebuked his disciples and indicated that they had much to learn from the openness and innocence—the natural purity of mind—of the little ones.

Another example of how our conventional ideas of goodness and humility can act as a barrier to our reception of the supreme wisdom, occurs at the Last Supper, when Jesus washes the feet of his disciples. We remember when he comes to Peter, Peter draws back and says: 'Thou shalt never wash my feet.'

To the conventional way of looking at things, Peter's response is admirable. The other disciples had allowed the Lord to make this supreme gesture, and surely it should have been the other way round—that they, as servants, washed the feet of him who was their supreme master. But in fact those disciples were right to accept without question whatever the Lord presented them with, and Peter was deluded in allowing his reasoning mind to enter into the situation and manage it according to his own limited understanding of virtue.

Jesus thus indicates that this clinging to a set of values, based on a belief in the reality and competence of our mind, is an obstacle that hinders us from identifying with the supreme truth—becoming a channel for that light. For truth never can reveal itself in the heart where there are buts, shoulds, questionings —a heart that is already filled. Therefore Jesus says to Peter: 'What I do, thou knowest not now... If I wash thee not, thou hast no part of me... Ye are clean—but not all.' (*John*, 13:4-10)

The rare quality of instantaneous acceptance of whatever comes to us from the highest spiritual source, is exemplified by Mary, mother of Christ. One instance occurs at the marriage feast in Cana, the scene of the first miracle recorded in the *Gospel of St John*—the transformation of the water into wine. Mary says to her son: 'They have no wine.' Jesus replies: 'Woman, what have I to do with thee?' Mary's response to this apparently harsh rebuff is simply to tell the servants that, as regards Jesus's words, 'Whatever he says to you, do it.' (*John*, 2:3-5)

At the end of this Gospel, the evangelist tells us that if he should relate everything that Jesus did, the world itself could not contain the books that should be written. This is because *sansara*—the world—for all its magnitude, is the realm of limitations, and the supreme truth is infinite consciousness—the absolute reality behind the changing appearances. The human mind, too, is a limited instrument, prone to error even when its motives are seemingly benevolent or spiritual. As Meister Eckhart comments in his sermon, 'The Good Hinders the Best', we tend to 'expend too much diligence on superfluous things and are never joined to the truth—for truth is to be found within and not in visible phenomena.'

It is only when we are willing to transcend the mind through submerging its activities in the being of our being, that the true quality of the light transmitted by Jesus will be revealed to us.

In the Book of Revelations we read: 'And behold I come quickly', because ultimately there is no distance or difference between Self and the supreme reality. In the end the seeker finds that he is the one sought, because 'the kingdom of heaven is within you'.

12

THE SHVETASHVATARA UPANISHAD

THE *SHVETASHVATARA* is an Upanishad imbued with the spirit of *bhakti* or devotion. It fuses together the deepest devotion to truth with the highest knowledge. This has immense practical value, since human beings are both intellectual and emotional, and both these aspects of our nature need to be trained and transformed. Emotion and intellect, heart and mind, can be united creatively in the same inner quest. When this happens, a great power is awakened within the personality.

The *Shvetashvatara* is thought to have appeared some centuries after the oldest Upanishads, perhaps around 200-300 BCE. In it we find ourselves in an atmosphere of impersonal, and hence universal, communication and teaching. No name is mentioned until the very end, when we are told that such were the teachings given by the sage, Shvetashvatara. Even this is an epithet rather than a name. It means White Mule, and may suggest that the teacher was a sage who rode a white mule. Thus the Upanishads encourage us to forget superficialities, and try to grasp the essence of what is being said.

To highlight our situation in the world, the Upanishad gives two vivid images. The first is that of a great wheel. (1:4) This is the wheel of sansara, the wheel of the world, which has innumerable sub-divisions, and the individual is caught in the motions of this wheel. The image suggests that our lives are driven by events and circumstances beyond our control. The Upanishad makes it clear that our own psychological forces—our emotions, our wishes, and so on—play their part in driving the motion of this wheel. But whatever the cause, our understanding, while revolving on this wheel, is extremely limited. We do not see the whole picture, and our desires and self-interest distort our understanding of our environment.

The verse about the wheel is followed by another image, that of a turbulent river, with strong currents and whirlpools in which the individual is caught. Again, the imprisoning force is not envisaged as entirely external: our own habits of sense, thought and desire make their contribution to what the Upanishad calls the tortuous and disturbing course of this river. (1:5)

The way to relief and freedom does exist, but it is a more subtle process than changing our physical circum-stances. This way of escape might better be called a way of outgrowth, leading to transcendence. It takes place, not on the outer plane, but on the inner one of the mind and its higher consciousness. The purpose of the Upanishads is to shed light on this path to transcendence.

It is of some interest that in this Upanishad, the wheel is not actually called the wheel of Sansara (repeated worldly existence). Instead, it is called the wheel of Brahman. Brahman is the Absolute, the supreme power, and it is said to sustain and nourish the wheel and the beings within it. Even on this wheel, therefore, there is an intimate link with the supreme reality. Our choice is either to get lost in the details of the wheel, confining our vision to our own particular spoke, or we can seek to know the ultimate mover of the wheel, the divine power. In a key verse (4:7), the Upanishad declares that the individual soul, feeling itself to be different from the supreme reality, suffers on this wheel. But when it realizes its essential identity with the ultimate controller of the wheel, then it knows itself to be free and immortal.

The *Shvetashvatara Upanishad* includes many prayers, expressing adoration and seeking help and support. Here the enlightened sage is setting an example of the right approach to the path to Self-realization, which will not yield its secrets to force or egoistic self-sufficiency. These prayers are like a thread running through this particular Upanishad. They have their climax in the great prayers for a clear understanding—for a pure intellect—that will be considered shortly. In none of the prayers is anything concrete sought in the outer world. Through them, we are encouraged to seek help in spiritual practice and for a deeper communion with the power underlying all. In this sense prayer is an attempt of our limited human mind to come into touch with the universal intelligence that sustains the world, and to become aware of its presence in our own heart.

This dimension of prayer links it with meditation, and also with the higher knowledge and understanding. It is an aspect of prayer that is easily forgotten in our busy life-style. A poem by James Russell Lowell indicates how rare true prayer is, and also points to the inner freedom that is available through such prayer:

> I, that still pray at morning and at eve...
> Thrice in my life perhaps have truly prayed,
> Thrice, stirred below my conscious self, have felt
> That perfect disenthralment which is God.

Disenthralment means freedom from bondage, and the poet, through such prayer, gained an insight into the nature of his own deeper Self.

Another theme of the *Shvetashvatara Upanishad* is the immanence, or omnipresence, of spiritual reality. Therefore we have such verses as:

> Thou art woman, thou art man,
> Thou art the youth and the maiden too.
> Thou art the old man tottering with a staff.
> Being born, thou becomest facing in every
> direction.

Thou art the dark-blue bird and the green parrot with
red eyes.
Thou hast the lightning as thy child.
Thou art the seasons and the seas.
Having no beginning, thou dost abide with immanence
From which all beings are born. (4:3-4)

Such verses suggest a reconciliation with the world of
appearances, a friendly and unified vision that knows
no fear, yet which also penetrates deeper.

The word immanence comes from the Latin verb
'manere' which means 'to remain'. The particular
forms do not remain, and the youth may well become
the old man tottering with a staff. The thoughts that
animate the mind of the youth, and also of the old man,
do not remain: they come and go. But something
deeper within all beings does remain. It can be called
the spiritual essence, and its nature is existence-
consciousness, and when truly understood, bliss. It not
only remains. It is the hidden support and ground of all,
and this is what the sage is aware of when he declares:
'Thou art the youth, the maiden, the seasons and the
seas.' There is the benevolent acceptance of appearances, yet all the time seeing beyond them.

This realization of ultimate truth is not just for the
gifted few. It is the culmination and goal of human
understanding. Enlightenment alone will bring about
the final fulfilment that all, consciously or unconscious-
ly, are seeking. The emphasis is on knowledge—of

something *known*, understood, realized. The answer to our problems lies not in our deeds or achievements, but in the quality of our knowledge. This has nothing to do with intellectual knowledge. As the poet, Jemshid, has written:

> There is in your soul a certain knowledge, which if you display it to mankind,
> They would tremble like a branch agitated by a strong wind.
> The choicest effulgence is the shining of knowledge on one endowed with understanding.

This is the knowledge awaiting discovery in each and everyone. Repeatedly, the *Shvetashvatara Upanishad* tells us: 'By knowing Him, one cuts the cords of death... By knowing God, one is released from all fetters.' And again:

> That God, whose work is this universe and who is all-pervasive, is ever present in the hearts of beings. He is the one who is framed by the heart, by the mind, by the thought. They who know That become immortal.

> His form is not to be beheld. No one sees Him with the eye. They who thus know Him, with heart and mind, as abiding in the heart, become immortal. (4:17 and 20)

In another verse, the Upanishad gives a metaphor to illustrate the point that lasting happiness depends on the realization of ultimate truth:

> When men will be able to roll up the sky like a piece of leather, only then will there be an end to sorrow— without knowing the Effulgent One. (6:20)

Thus our attention is being directed towards something extremely near, something framed, so to speak, by our very thought—present in our heart. But how can we become sensitive to this level of our being, and prove to ourselves its authenticity?

Within the *Shvetashvatara Upanishad* there is a group of verses recommending the practice of meditation with the aim of self-transcendence. Meditation is an attempt to still the normal thinking processes and rest the attention on a theme that points beyond limitations, such as the Self as pure consciousness. Once some degree of inner silence is achieved, we sustain our focus on what is there at the heart of our being, and this leads to the recognition that the Self transcends individuality. Central to this development is the emergence of what the Upanishad calls a 'pure intellect'. This is indicated in one of its great prayers:

> The One, who himself without colour,
> by the manifold application of His power,
> Distributes many colours in His hidden purpose,

And into whom, its end and its beginning, the whole
world dissolves: He is God.
May He endow us with pure intellect. (4:1)

The prayer affirms the transcendental nature of the
supreme by calling it 'the One without colour'. It also
denotes the mystery and wonder of the world of appearances, with its extraordinary range of colours that
surpasses anything that can be depicted by the greatest
of artists. The purpose of all this play is said to be
beyond human understanding. The prayer then focuses
on the quality of human understanding itself, by
praying for a pure intellect. Such an intellect, it is
implied, will have access to the deeper mysteries of
life, and will lead the way to enlightenment.

It may be asked, that if one is going to pray for
spiritual help at all, why not pray for enlightenment
itself? Should we not be encouraged to pray for Self-
realization, which is the ultimate goal? Why not ask for
it directly?

As certain verses of the Upanishad have revealed,
from the standpoint of ultimate truth, our reality *is* the
Absolute, so, in the deepest sense, we already are That
which we aspire to, and we stand where we seek to be.
To pray for enlightenment is to perpetuate the error that
enlightenment is far from us. It is like praying on a
cloudy day for the sun to come to the sky. The fact is

that the sun is already in the sky, to be revealed when the clouds disperse.

The meaning of a pure intellect is an awakened intuitive faculty. This has nothing necessarily to do with intellectual ability. It means an intellect that is sensitive to the deeper power of consciousness at its source. To prepare the mind for the awakening and maturing of this faculty, an inner clearing is necessary. It requires deliberate forgetfulness of our individuality in quest of something deeper and greater. This involves developing a wider view, learning not to take personally everything that happens to or around us, so that it hurts or flatters our pride. It is an ability to stand back from our own personality, and, if necessary, to subdue its self-assertion and redirect its trend. In this way, higher aspects of our intellect, which relate to our ultimate nature, will begin to stir.

The *Shvetashvatara Upanishad* compares this process to the cleaning of a golden disc that has been silted up with thick earth. (2:14) As the earth is peeled off, and the surface is washed and polished, the disc reveals its splendour and its power to reflect the light. Similarly, through the practices, an inner clarification will take place, and we will be gifted with insights about our deeper Self.

The purification of our intellect is a process of self–discovery, that has to be pursued with interest, love and trust. Past habits do not quickly drop away, and progress usually comes in slow stages, step by step.

Besides, our intellect is bombarded on all sides by distractions that keep us in a state of restlessness and tension. Few cherish solitude or can appreciate that it has any value at all. Silence, inner or outer, is seen by many as a condition to be avoided. And yet, the purification of the intellect requires a willingness to forget the world and its details for a time, and also to forget the picture of ourselves that we have built up during our lives.

Another image given in the Upanishad is that of churning milk to get butter, butter being traditionally regarded as the most delicious essence of the milk. (1:15-16) Here the milk stands for the mind, and the butter for the peace and light that we are seeking. As with milk, the butter does not just appear, even if we want it to. The milk has to be churned, that is, given a thorough stirring, and if this is done patiently, the butter will emerge. The path laid down in the Upanishads is a comprehensive course of inner trans-formation, which brings out the best in us, and clears aside all tendencies that stand as obstacles to our enlightenment.

Any teaching that intimates that our true Self is immortal and infinite needs to be approached with caution. There are serious possibilities of misunder-standing the upanishadic doctrines. The true Self, in ordinary experience, appears to be mixed up with the mental consciousness, although it is in fact free and transcendent, and is the innermost principle of awareness. It can never be the property of any individual, since it is the revealing light that illumines all bodies and minds equally. The need to transcend the ego is denoted in the last verse of this classical text, which returns to the theme of devotion, or *bhakti*, and its range is extended to include the spiritual teacher, or guru (6:23):

> He who has supreme devotion to the Lord, and to his Guru as to the Lord, to him indeed is revealed the real meaning of the truths declared in this Upanishad.

A guru is considered an essential aid to anyone wishing to complete the path of light. From wisdom based on personal experience, a guru can help the enquirer in innumerable ways, and point the pupil in the right direction at every stage. A true guru does not promote his or her own personality, nor exploit those who come for instruction, but is a well-wisher in every sense.

This does not mean that one should postpone one's quest until one has found a guru. One can begin the life of spiritual endeavour straight away, through practice and right aspiration. Our ultimate guru is the supreme reality, and that reality is ever present as our true Self. There will be a response to our sincerity whether or not we are aware of it. If we pursue our quest, our understanding will deepen, our confidence and trust in this guidance will be strengthened, and we will be led to make the right decisions.

Once we have prepared ourselves and the time is ripe, the guru will find us, or, more precisely, we will have the discernment to recognize a true guru. A knower of truth is inwardly free, and has the purity and insight to recognize our hidden capacities, and also to see the inner obstacles that are preventing these capacities from flowering. One meaning of the word 'guru' is 'remover of darkness', that is, a remover of the impediments to our inner illumination. Such a one has gone beyond personality and is identified with truth itself. So when the Upanishad recommends devotion to the teacher as to God, it is not to the personality of the teacher, but to one who has found the way to inner freedom, who is perfectly fulfilled and can lead a sincere seeker to that freedom and lasting fulfilment.

13

DISCOVERING THE
BRIGHT PEARL WITHIN

Why should you look for treasure abroad?
Within yourself you have the bright pearl.

Pao-Chih

THESE WORDS are taken from a hymn composed by a Buddhist priest who lived in fifth century China. Each of us holds a pearl, luminous, perfect, indestructible, and that is our true Self. But like the attempt to secure a pearl before it is recovered from its oyster shell clinging to the sea's bed, we have to go deeper into ourselves to benefit fully from our hidden wealth. This is achieved by means of meditation, cultivating serenity in daily life, and taking an ever deeper interest in our quest for Self-knowledge.

Why is it that we do not experience directly the life-giving power and peace at the core of our being? It is because most of us are content with what we find on the surface of life. Mystical poets like Kabir urge us:

The pearl is in the oyster,
And the oyster is at the bottom of the sea.
Dive deep; give up love of life!

Kabir can sound severe, because there is nothing wrong in loving life. Actually, those who pursue wisdom love life more deeply and meaningfully than those who make life serve their narrow self-interest. The seeker of truth senses something miraculous and purposeful in the whole experience of living. If we want to come into touch with the beauty that never fades and the peace that never wanes, we have to dive deeper into ourselves, and approach, so to say, the divine pearl of truth at the core of our being.

Our intellect is a wonderful, world-shaping faculty. But as regards the higher wisdom, calmness of heart counts for more than cleverness of mind. A man once approached the Sufi master, Jalaluddin Rumi, and said, in effect: 'Science tells us so much about man—his nature, his temperament, and so on. Yet it sheds no light on whether there is anything in our nature that is immortal.' Rumi replied: 'If this knowledge could be yours through question and answer, it would be worth very little. There has to be a different approach.' And he goes on: 'A man comes to the sea, and sees nothing but water, sharks and fishes. He says: "Where is this pearl they speak about? Perhaps there isn't any pearl." How should the pearl be attained by looking at the sea?... A diver is needed to discover the pearl—a diver who has skill and luck.'

'There has to be a different approach.' Our approach to conscious immortality is very different from our normal advance in knowledge. It depends on learning how to still and purify the sea that stirs within us, our mind. We may object: 'But if I make my mind quiet, I will know less. Perhaps I will know nothing at all.' This is a mistake. A calm mind, well-informed about the doctrine of the true Self, symbolized by the pearl, will reveal to us that pearl. We will gain a new understanding that satisfies and fulfils us.

It is true that in the world of nature you have to be lucky to find a pearl. Not every stretch of sea has an oyster bed, and not every oyster develops a pearl. But in our quest for self–realization, each of us shares the same starting-point and the same end-point: that our fundamental nature transcends limitations, and we are in this world to realize it. Through practising the higher yoga, we stand to gain much in the way of internal stability and balance, a deeper power of comprehension, and the blessing of inner peace.

On this no-lose situation, the *Bhagavad Gita* encourages us: 'Here there is no wasted effort, here there is no harm; even a little of this yoga protects us from great fear.'—that is, it adds to our sense of peace and security. Yoga is not like farming, where there is a risk of crop failure, hence unrewarded effort; and it is not like medicine, which sometimes has unfortunate side-effects. The idea is, if even a little yoga can help, how much more rewarding will be regular practice.

DISCOVERING THE BRIGHT PEARL WITHIN

A metaphor, like that of the bright pearl within, teaches indirectly, poetically, through suggestion. But it may not be clear what it is pointing to. We are seeking a direct way to self-discovery. So let us be direct. The pearl is the divine principle within us, our true Self, our 'I'. It seems to be identified with the mind as our ego, and this ego takes itself most seriously, intensifying our sense of individuality and our feeling of separateness and isolation.

But this ego is no pearl. It is a part of the mind. And the hidden support of mind and ego is the real Self, the infinite 'I', which transcends all boundaries and is not separate from anything. 'Atman is one with Param-atman'—our innermost Self is one with the supreme Self of the universe, and there is only one Self. When the mystics speak of being one with the divine, it is their deeper Self that knows itself to be infinite; and, as for the ego-self, it is transcended in the fullness of this new understanding.

When the word 'I' is used in texts for meditation, it points directly to our infinite nature. But before awakening to Self-knowledge, our mind has to be carefully and sensitively prepared, so that we are established in such qualities as equanimity, harmless-ness and singleness of purpose. Our intellectual discipline involves the development of the faculty of discrimination, *viveka*. This is the capacity to discern what the Self is not—to distinguish between the

171

changing phenomena and the unchanging consciousness that illumines all experience.

The 'I' that we are trying to discover is our true Self, and it is transcendent. It does not have any worldly qualities, physical or mental, material or subtle. The Self, which is the light behind our thoughts, is a mystery because it allows our individuality to appear, as it were, and also allows itself to be concealed by that individuality. It is the power of the real Self that is the reality underlying our appearance. Yet in itself, the Self transcends all appearances. No wonder the intellect cannot grasp it through question and answer, but it can approach the true Self, the ground of being, through stillness and an interior attentive silence.

What about the mind? Sometimes the mind is spoken of as the main barrier to an illumined understanding. We may be told that its restless activity stands in the way of our realization, that it keeps us in bondage with its desires and fears, that it leads us on with false promises, and that it opposes our spiritual advance, because it wants above all to retain its power and influence over us.

But there is also a case for saying that this mind of ours, even in our state of unenlightenment, really wants to be our friend and helper; that its whole function is to please and protect us. For example, if we look at our spontaneous reactions in almost any circumstance, they are so often to do with securing our pleasure or our safety. The mind instantly calculates: 'This will bring me joy; this will make me feel better'; or, 'I don't want that—it poses a threat.' We could say that almost every motion of the mind has something of this calculation running through it. The mind wants us to be happy and safe. How can it be our enemy?

The key question is not whether the mind is our enemy or friend, but why even when the mind is at its friendliest towards us, even when it fills us with worldly joy, we still do not feel one hundred per cent safe and fulfilled? If our mind has been trying to help us all this time—our lifetime—why this enduring restlessness? Why does one desire lead to another, and why is true happiness always on the horizon and never under our feet?

The answer is that the mind can help to lead us out of our difficulties, but it needs to be tutored in the way of wisdom and enlightenment. On the negative side, it still has not learnt that 'Whatever fades, but fading pleasure brings'. So there is a chance that experience will prompt us to awaken through disappointments.

But more than this, the mind seems to be unaware of the free nature that underlies it. It needs to be informed that there is a true Self, and also initiated in the methods through which we may awaken to the higher Self-knowledge. Part of this education involves the clear recognition that the pleasure and safety we are looking for are to be found within, not outside. And then these advantages will no longer be called pleasure and safety, but take on new and more appropriate names: bliss (*ananda*) and fearlessness (*nirbhaya*), based on the true completion and fulfilment of our longings. For Self-realization alone will bring about the satisfactory closure of the mind's long search for lasting happiness.

It is said that the things of the world are gained with difficulty, kept with anxiety and lost with anguish. There is enjoyment in ordinary life, as long as we can avoid getting desperate about our position or our relationships, and stay even-minded as we pass through life. But there is greater enjoyment if we realize the limitations of the search for outer happiness, and seek the bright pearl within our own being. The highest good available to us arises from the depth of our soul and from nowhere else.

There is a story by John Steinbeck, called *The Pearl.* A poor fisherman spends part of his time diving for pearls. The oyster beds are not far down, but you need clear water and excellent breath control to choose the best oysters for plucking. One day, Kito, for that is his name, glimpses what seems to be the sheen of a large pearl, peeping through the shell divide. And it turns out to be a pearl the size of a seagull's egg—the greatest pearl in the world. But, and we can guess it, the possession of this pearl starts a train of appalling problems, as eyes turn green around him, and his situation becomes life-threatening. The story shows how, in the world, whether our aims are simple and innocent, or selfish and villainous, consequences escape our control, and often burden us with unanticipated worries or anxieties.

What we really want is safety, happiness, fearlessness and fulfilment, with no hidden impediments. And these are all enshrined within us. The quest for wisdom and enlightenment is a safe one, coveting nothing, envying none, and willing to learn by following the guidelines of the great masters of the path.

Perhaps we can now widen the metaphor to indicate the practical implications of following the path of Self–discovery. The sea is the mind, the pearl is the true I, the immortal Self. And the oyster is like the faculty of pure intuition which develops in the mind as we pursue the way of Self-knowledge.

Every man and woman possesses the latent capacity to grow in wisdom and know the supreme truth of 'I', and be free. This is our birthright as human beings. The faculty of perfect wisdom is dormant in every intellect. It is awakened when our mind works on itself through the practice of the higher yoga. It has been called the supra-conscious mind, and holds within itself the power of transcendent knowledge, as the shell holds the pearl. This faculty is itself subject to expansion, until recognition dawns; then its function, and the work of the mind, have found completion.

Our striving for joy in the world is a sign that we are made for joy; but we need to be connoisseurs, experts, in this matter, and not naive victims of false suggestions. The real purveyors of joy are the knowers of truth. They have no private motive, because they have replaced personal egoism with the knowledge: 'There is only one Self in all, and that am I.'

Our true Self is eternal and infinite, and we all can realize this truth within us. We need never be discouraged by the chaos or dejection we may find in our mental life. The mind is not the real I. Nor should we be dismayed at the changes that we experience in our physical body. Our original being is never touched by change or decay. It is ever pristine and perfect. The Taoist poet Han Shan reminds us of the way of wisdom:

> Though face and form alter with the years,
> I hold fast to the pearl of the mind.

If we are steadfast in this quest, we will realize that the goal we seek is the true nature of the one who seeks it.

14

THE COMPLETE LIFE

WHAT IS the complete life? The fulfilment of enlightenment, where we know in direct experience that our true Self is infinite, immortal, ever at peace, ever satisfied. The attainment of this completeness has more to do with our state of mind than with the comfort or prosperity of our outer situation. For, as life teaches us every day, there is no guarantee of security in our outer affairs. Life is a manifestation of the ever-moving stream of *sansara*. However competent we may be in managing our life, we can only control things up to a certain point.

But as for our inner life—the world within the mind—this is a realm we can transform and uplift if we have the desire and will to do so. Following safe and traditional guidelines, we will be led ultimately to Self-realization and complete understanding—the certainty that we have fulfilled the purpose of life.

We may ask: 'How then can we experience such a complete life?' This wholeness is already an accomplished fact within us. It is the true nature of our being, the reality behind our appearance, the power behind our mind. What is it that roots us in a sense of limitation and imperfection? It is our way of thinking—the totality of thoughts, ideas, opinions, desires and anxieties we have accumulated as we have developed.

These generate our strong conviction that we are identified with our body, mind and senses, and are nothing more. The complete life is the expression of our reality, free from the influence of these fluctuations of the mind.

The way of progress and inner revelation is through transforming our mind into a source of peace and higher understanding. To do this, we need to become aware of all the forces in our personality and turn them into our helpers, not impediments.

Broadly speaking, the means to a complete life are:

1   A way of action that creates and expresses harmony within and around us, and frees us from anxiety.

2   A way of satisfying our emotions that expresses the wholeness of our being.

3   A way of intelligence that leads us from intellectual knowledge to the wisdom of inner light.

Let us first consider the nature of action and how best to act in pursuit of our goal. Often our actions have unforeseen consequences, and the unfolding of those consequences becomes our destiny. In the classical texts, actions are classified threefold: of body, speech and mind. All actions which are purposefully under-taken produce effects in our own being and in the world around us. This fact about human nature is attributed to a great law, the law of karma, which is expressed in the saying: 'As ye sow, so shall ye reap'. Such consequences are held to be inevitable, either in the short or longer term. Our actions, therefore, have their 'reward'. If they spring from self-interest, they consolidate our sense of individuality—of being 'a doer and enjoyer' identified with our body, mind and personality. This in itself is a limitation on consciousness, which veils from us the freedom of our true Self.

Is there a way of acting which not only protects us from making karmic mistakes, but also leads to our complete freedom from the bonds of action?

What we have to do is to widen our understanding in order to recognize that we are not really imprisoned in our individuality, but are part of the great all-knowing Whole. How we name that supreme principle is for us to decide. We may call it the ultimate source, the 'Dharmic body of the Buddha', or Brahman, or God, or the cosmic mind. But if we can do our actions as an offering to this universal power that is the source of our own being, we will discover the path to inner freedom.

This way of action means that we are doing our best, but our happiness and peace of mind are no longer dependent on the results. If things do not go according to plan, we will be spared the feelings of self-pity or self-blame. If we are successful, we will not be carried away by self-glory. Our practice is rooted in equanimity; the even-mindedness we associate with meditation is extended to our life of action and response in the world. It is then that the consequences will lose the power of binding us, because our psychological point of reference will be our higher mind, which is free from the self-interest of the ego.

One way of self-upliftment is to try to forget our narrow self-interest and to lose ourselves in what we are doing, for its own sake. This creates, as it were, an aperture in our mind, and gives us a sense of inner freedom. The possibility of transcendence through self-forgetfulness, however short-lived, is recognized by the poet T S Eliot when he writes of:

> ... music heard so deeply
> That it is not heard at all, but you are the music
> While the music lasts.*

Through this self-forgetting concentration, the duality of hearer and heard, thinker and thought, doer and what is being done, is momentarily dissolved. The ideal is action without egoism, and without being distracted by thoughts of past or future.

In practice we will find it effective to offer consciously what we do, to this great underlying power

* From 'The Dry Salvages'. *Collected Poems 1909-1962*. These lines and those quoted on page 182 are reproduced with permission of the publisher, Faber and Faber Ltd.

that ultimately moves and rules the world. For example: 'I offer this work, and also this leisure or entertainment, to You. May my mind stay tranquil and may nothing hinder my spiritual progress.' It is up to the individual to express this in their own way. The *Bhagavad Gita* has many verses on this liberating way of acting:

> Those who perform their duty without attachment, surrendering the results to the supreme reality, are not affected by sinful action, as the petals of a lotus are untouched by water. (5:10)

The aim is to live in the world, as we must, but not be entirely of the world. A similar image from the Taoist writings is that we have to live and move in the world as a boat moves on water. What is important is to make sure the water stays under the boat and does not fill it. It is the same with life. If we can do our actions in this free and unselfish way, our mind will be relieved of a host of unnecessary and largely self-created cares and concerns.

Once we can accept that there is this trancendent dimension of our being, and that we are attuning our mind to this infinite Presence, we find that we are establishing a relationship that has deep implications, and where there is no real dividing line between us and the supreme reality.

Nowadays relationship is celebrated more than ever, through social networking and our love of being in touch. This suggests that most people feel a need to be in constant communion with others. On the other hand, we do not want our relationships to be hollow and superficial. This shallowness is also described by Eliot in his poem, 'The Hollow Men', which begins:

> We are the hollow men
> We are the stuffed men
> Leaning together
> Headpiece filled with straw. Alas!

There is one relationship which is deep, pure, ever unfolding, ever expanding. And this is possible if we have the conviction that our life is linked with the infinite, and will finally reveal itself as nothing other than the infinite. In the words of the Sufi master, Rumi,

> He is a lover of the Universal, and he himself is the Universal: he is in love with himself and seeking his own love.   (*Mathnawi*, Book I, 1574)

This identification is the ultimate fruit of the fusion of our individual consciousness with the universal consciousness to which we have learnt to offer our actions. This way of living and acting will prove such a relief that we will naturally wish to draw nearer to that deeper reality with a sense of devotion.

Here too we find a way to be helped—emotionally. As we know, there is no more unsettling force in the mind than the desires that rise in us and demand our attention and submission. The desiring habit has held sway throughout our human evolution and is indispensable for our life in the world. But as human beings we have an option. Our mind not only desires but has the power to choose what to desire. One great desire, which is the opposite of the hollow and superficial, is the urge for deeper communion and identity with the infinite.

We may say: 'This is impossible. How can the finite mind desire the infinite?' And yet there is something deep in human nature that has an affinity with the infinite. This principle is intimately present in our being, but it is more inward and subtle than the mental life. Being pure awareness, it knows the mind from within—not as one of the mind's faculties, but as an interior vantage point that transcends the mind. This is the infinite in us seeking, one might say, to realize its true nature as infinity, just as the space in a jar, if it were conscious, may seek to realize its true identity as the universal space.

As the infinite has no form, it is not easy for the human mind to connect with something so subtle, abstract and universal. And so we are given symbols of the infinite, ideas and images that our mind can grasp and which attract us and absorb our attention. Symbols are not ends in themselves. Their ultimate aim is to lead us beyond all qualities to the realization of the ineffable reality which is symbolized and is our true nature. To give some examples: a saint or a sage we admire may be a symbol—a focus of our attention; or we may be drawn to an incarnation of God who inspires our reverence and devotion. A word of power like peace, light or OM may be a symbol. Even a philosophical world view, like Vedanta, is an extended symbol, pointing to a deeper reality. What is symbolized in all cases is the Infinite, the One, the source, and these symbols are not meant to be walls that limit our range and aspiration, but windows through which we may discern that same infinite reality.

We mentioned before that there is an element in us which transcends the mind, which is the infinite trying, as it were, to realize itself through our Self-realization. This is why the completeness of being is already an accomplished fact within us. It is a new way of understanding, and not a fundamental change in our nature, that will open the inner door. Once we can appreciate how to live in the world in tune with the infinite, and how to liberate our feelings from what is superficial and narrow, our ultimate guide will be our thirst for the supreme knowledge.

We all have a need to know, and, if we are seeking the complete life, we will not rest content until our faculty of cognition—of knowledge—is satisfied for ever. And we are most fortunate if we have this divine discontent. What we are seeking is what is nearest to us. It is inseparable from our ultimate being as 'I am'. This is our true Self, the Atman. It is not that we possess it. In a sense, it possesses us, being superior to all. But it is as if we have become unmindful of it. The true meaning of mindfulness—the deepest meaning—is to be mindful of what we are.

Can we attain our own Self? Is the word 'attain' appropriate? In one sense, it is valid. If we feel incomplete, we have, as it were, to attain to completeness through effort. If we feel we do not know ourselves in this perfect way, we need to attain the knowledge, and so enlightenment becomes our 'goal'. But in a deeper sense, our goal is ever achieved. When we try to attain, we place it at an artificial distance. We set up an image in our mind, something which is actually different from what we are.

The goal of our endeavours is ever attained. It is the completeness of our being, even now. Our challenge is to realize this, not create it. The step we are preparing ourselves for is to transcend our current experience of our self as rooted in limitations and transience, and realize the Self as infinite consciousness.

In the Chinese Zen (or 'Chan') tradition there is a story about a monk who went to a Master and asked about the true meaning of illumination. The Master answered: 'Not to attain, not to know'. It goes back to the idea that when we try to attain to illumination—to completeness—we delusively place it at a distance. The monk then asked: 'Is there some turning point in going beyond, or not?' In other words, some step or steps must be needed, because it seems to be the case that we human beings are not completely fulfilled—that we are not at rest in the bliss of Self-realization. Something must be necessary. In answer to this, the Master said: 'The vast sky does not hinder white clouds from flying.'

The teaching is that the glory of our true nature—absolute consciousness, limitless and free—is not in conflict with our mental states or our body-consciousness, any more than the infinite sky is in conflict with the clouds that sail in it. Realization is the withdrawal of our sense of identity from the limitations of our individuality to the unbounded freedom of consciousness absolute. It is not an attainment, not something to be known as different from ourselves, but the realization of the eternal completeness of our being.

We may be told that the complete life is to do good and make a difference to the outer world as best we can. As human beings we need to be caring, co-operative, friendly, open, sincere and generous-hearted. But such a life will flourish only if our mind is open to the inner light and peace of true wisdom.

The spiritual Yoga rests on something deeper than conventional ideas of virtue. It helps us to consciously bond our inner being with that in us which is the fountainhead of all goodness and truth. And we do this by merging our limited consciousness with the supreme consciousness through the yogic way of action, feeling and knowledge. With our mind thus transformed, we may be active in the world or live a more retired life. In either case, we will be a channel through which good flows unselfishly and spontaneously for the peace and upliftment of all.

15

THE OPEN SECRET OF THE UPANISHADS

'I am lighting a lamp to dispel the dark illusion that
covers the heart of humanity.'

THESE WORDS, attributed to the ancient seer, Vyasa,
apply equally well to the purpose and work of Shri
Shankara. The main point of Shankara's teaching on
Self-knowledge is to awaken us to the realization that
our innermost self is the sole reality of the universe,
and that any other conception of self is based on an
illusion at the core of our experience—an illusion that
will be dispelled when we light the lamp of spiritual
wisdom in our heart.

This philosophy explains that our present experience
of the world, feeling ourselves to be separate and
vulnerable, identified with a limited organ of experience, the mind, is a kind of error, a mistake. The
reality is not this bittersweet experience yielded by the
mind and the senses, nor is it the multiplicity of things
we see within and around us, like the multiplicity of
waves on the surface of the sea. Ultimate truth transcends the world. It is immutable, ever pure, perfect,
denoted in the Upanishads as 'one only without a
second' and one with our own essential Self, just as the
reality of the waves is only water.

This is the secret doctrine (*rahasya*) hidden in the heart of the Upanishads, called Advaita or non-duality. It is also the main message of the *Bhagavad Gita*, where this great realization is approached in various ways through the purification of the mind. At every step, Shankara shows that this is meant to be a practical philosophy, a practical path of re-educating our intellect, emotions and will. It is not a philosophy in the speculative sense, but a seeing of things as they really are, without the illusions that are created and upheld by our imagination.

Its practical side is called Adhyatma Yoga, the Yoga of Self-knowledge, a range of practices and a way of life that is intended to lead our understanding to 'direct experience of reality', or, in the words of an ancient prayer, that we may be led 'from error to truth, from darkness to light, from death to immortality.' This prayer is to be taken as a statement of practical purpose, the very purpose of our life in this world as intelligent conscious beings. It is fulfilled by seeing through the mystery of our own consciousness and being, and this is the real field of Shankara's philosophy, which is transmitted and unfolded in the course of his comments on the ancient revealed texts.

Let us consider the question: 'What am I?' In the collection of Shankara's writings called *The Thousand Teachings*, we find the answer to this question presented in direct and uncompromising terms. For example:

> I am the Lord, ever one and the same in all beings, beyond the destructible and indestructible principles, hence the supreme Spirit. Although I am the supreme Self and one without a second, I am mistakenly supposed to be other than this on account of nescience.*

> I am the Self, entirely pure, without a veil, unaffected by nescience or its false suggestions or by actions and their results. Though (apparently) clothed in the powers of sight, hearing, etc., I am one without a second, eternally fixed in my own true nature, motionless like the ether of the sky.

> I am the Self, the supreme Absolute, pure consciousness am I, ever without a second, other than name, form and action, ever liberated by nature.

> (10:8-9 and 11:7)

Our progress in wisdom is reflected in our evolving conception of the supreme being and our relationship with it. At first this supreme principle is thought of as

* Nescience, or metaphysical ignorance, signifies our unawareness of the ultimate truth of the non-dual, absolute nature of the Self, accompanied by our conviction of the reality of the world of multiplicity.

the great power that rules the universe, separate from our own being, and worshipped as He or That. On deepening acquaintance, so to say, the pronoun changes, and this power is addressed as You, or Thou, as found in the religious literature of all traditions. But the final stage is to recognize that point of light and consciousness in our own being, in other words, our I, when distinguished from all that is changeable in us, as the same divine principle that we formerly worshipped as other.

This doctrine, which is a veiled secret in some traditions, which is generally spoken of in guarded terms by the mystics of Christianity and Islam, is the starting point of Shri Shankara's philosophy. It is not only presented openly, but shown to be reasonable and an elucidation of our own experience. Through reasoning, Shri Shankara shows how any other view of human nature is invalid because of the contradictions implicit in that view, or because it does not account for the whole of human experience.

At first sight, nothing could sound more unreasonable than to affirm that the true Self of a mere human is identical with the supreme reality. It should be noted that this is not speaking of a special type of person, but of our nature in general. This truth is, so to say, the pearl that is hidden in the oyster shell of our personality. What is the source of our knowledge of this truth? For this we have to go back to the

Upanishads. Here we find there are certain short statements, which proclaim this identity, and then we find many other verses in which this identity is stated or implied in more expanded terms.

One of these key utterances is found in the *Brihadaranyaka Upanishad*: 'I am Brahman', *Aham Brahmasmi* in Sanskrit. Brahman here means the Absolute, the ultimate Spirit, the All, God in the highest sense. We are considering a text which goes back centuries before Christ, and almost certainly predates the Buddha and the philosophical flowering in ancient Greece. The passage that contains this utterance is too profound to be readily understood and still retains its aura of sublimity; few statements can be so direct in their utterance of the highest truth.

> This (Self) was indeed Brahman in the beginning. It knew only itself as 'I am Brahman'. Therefore It became all. And whoever among the gods knew It, also became That. And the same with sages and men...To this day, whoever in like manner knows It as 'I am Brahman' becomes all this (universe). Even the gods cannot prevail against him, for he becomes their Self. While he who worships another god, thinking 'He is one, I am another', does not know.
>
> (*Brihadaranyaka Upanishad* 1:4:10)

Brahman itself, being the Absolute, is beyond the range of human thought, and can only be apprehended through the awakening of a higher faculty of Self-knowledge which comes to light in a condition of inner stillness, brought about through the dedicated pursuit and practice of the spiritual life. It is That 'from which the universe came forth, in which it abides, and into which it is finally dissolved'. The universe is held to be an appearance of Brahman, not ultimately real in itself. Though Brahman is undetected by the human senses, if it were not present as the underlying reality, nothing would exist. There is nothing outside Brahman, the Infinite, and it has no internal divisions or parts. The Upanishads speak of it as 'That', and all conceptions of God are tentative means to approach the reality of Brahman, yet while these remain conceptions, however sublime or subtle, they can never embrace the ultimate source of being, Brahman. Hence the Upanishads warn the enquirer that Brahman is 'not this, not this'—*neti, neti.* Yet, far from being an emptiness or a negation, Brahman is the source of all our experience, empirical and spiritual, and is 'greater than the great'.

Then we return to the question, 'What is this 'I' in us, this apparent centre of identity which provides our individual selfhood?' What right have we to equate it with the infinite, nameless, sublime principle indicated, not defined, through the language of the Upanishads? First, we ourselves are encouraged to investigate the nature of the 'I', through learning to expand our powers of reflection and introvertive penetration. This we can only do through a training in tranquillity and inward alertness. When we make this investigation, we encounter what might be called the mystery of consciousness.

Normally we think of consciousness as a quality associated with our physical and mental functions. When we are seeing, consciousness is involved in helping us to see, in making the visual experience possible; when we are hearing, or listening, again, consciousness is necessary to uphold these functions. It is the same with speech, and all our other faculties.

Even as we go deeper within ourselves, away from the sense life, into our inner world of thoughts and feelings, consciousness seems to play an essential part in the experience. It is always there, but somehow not noteworthy in itself. It only seems meaningful when manifest through certain recognisable functions.

But there is deeper light to be shed on this aspect of our experience. Another of the great upanishadic utterances is: 'Consciousness is Brahman'—*Prajnanam Brahman*. This in turn gives us an insight into the meaning of the statement: 'I am Brahman'. Because, if we ask, where God is in human nature, the answer is: God is the very consciousness in us. In other words, it is consciousness which in the end will show us that we are not 'only human', for our true nature is consciousness absolute, and there is no 'self' apart from That.

For one who has this realization, this infinite and non-dual nature of the true Self is the only valid experience. It is beyond the range of the mind. However, through enquiry, through carefully examining our own internal experience we can, up to a certain point, determine what the Self is not.

It was noted before that when we are seeing, hearing, thinking, feeling, and so on, consciousness is indispensable in making these functions possible. And yet we never actually *see* consciousness at work, we never *hear* its presence, and we never *think* 'consciousness' as a thought. What, then, is the nature of our innermost consciousness?

Let us consider a particular aspect of our internal experience. Evidently, as human beings, we are aware of our thoughts. There is a sense in which our thoughts are seen by us, or by a principle of awareness within us. We may not be conscious of this awareness all the time. It may spring on us, for instance, in moments of embarrassment, when we become uncomfortably conscious of our own thoughts; or when we are unable to sleep because we cannot stop worrying about something; or as an awareness of distractions when we are trying to meditate. But whether we remain consciously aware of our thoughts or not, from the point of view of this introvertive enquiry, thoughts are part of what is seen. And since we only deduce that we have a mind from the evidence of thoughts and thinking, we can extend this by saying that the mind and its thoughts are part of the seen. They are not the Seer.

If we pursue this line of enquiry, we will come to realize that the mind and its thoughts are very different in nature from the principle of awareness or consciousness that witnesses them. For one thing, the thoughts are always moving and changing. They belong to a realm that is by nature perishable. Our thoughts share the same perishable nature as the material world that is usually their content.

But does this perishability apply to the conscious Seer of the thoughts? We cannot say so, because the Seer never actually appears as a thought. Does the Seer of the thoughts ever change? We cannot say so, because the Seer is never in an observable position where we can say: 'O yes, it has changed.' The Seer can never be the seen, and its awareness remains unalterable and unfailing.

The truth is that this ultimate Seer, this principle of awareness in us, is not only constant throughout our lifetime, but remains the same, untainted, unmoved, free, deathless, throughout all time. This dimension of our being transcends mind and matter, time and space, and it is identical with our consciousness.

This reasoning proves that our innermost consciousness is radically different in kind from anything else. For it is a changeless and subjective principle that can never be pointed to as a changing object. It is totally unlike the mind, which is finite in its operations and changes every moment.

There is in us the transcendent consciousness, and there is the rest of our make-up, which includes everything we are aware of. When the Upanishads use the expression quoted earlier, '*Neti neti*, not this, not this', they are speaking of the rest, that is, of all the objective elements in our experience. Whether we regard these as mental or material, all these phenomena, all these appearances, belong to the known, the seen, what can be talked about, what can be categorized, what we can make theories about. But the words '*Neti, neti*', never refer to the Seer, the Consciousness itself, because *Prajnanam Brahman*—Consciousness is Brahman.

From this simple fact of our inner experience—the fact that there is an all-seeing consciousness which never changes, and that there is a seen world of mind and matter that is always in a state of flux—Shri Shankara draws the most penetrating conclusion about the whole of our experience in this world. He explains how it cannot be accepted as real, or, if it is accepted as real, it is due to a mistake, an error that appears to work outwards from the very root of experience, but which has no logical validity, nor any validity from the standpoint of the supreme realization. This is because our experience is based on an apparent mingling of this innermost conscious light of awareness, which is constant and unalterable, with the ever-changing phenomena of the mind and its thoughts and faculties. The two principles are as different as light and darkness.

The conscious element in us is light, unalterable light, since it is the revealer of everything else in experience. Whereas the mind, with its continuous alteration, is compared to darkness. It gains its animation and apparent light and life from the presence of that ultimate light of the innermost consciousness, the true I, which both reveals thought and makes it possible. But is this play of consciousness, mind and matter really possible and, if so, how?

The supreme light of consciousness, the light of 'I', can have nothing in common with the realm of change, the realm of phenomena. Light cannot mix or fuse with darkness; you cannot make a structure of fire and snow. What is 'I', consciousness, cannot go into partnership with anything material to bring about a world experience. What is 'I', consciousness, as the ever-fixed subject, our immediate awareness, cannot step down and become part of the seen phenomena, part of the mind. It is a logical impossibility.

The mind is, as it were, a 'you', that is, something set apart from the true 'I'. It is, we could say, a 'you over there', compared with the inner light of awareness, that is the true 'I' or *aham* which is always our immediate experience. And yet this impossible mixing of subject and object, of Self and not-Self, of consciousness and the non-conscious, of eternal un-changing reality and the ever-changing appearances, of the true 'I' and the 'you', the mind; this apparent fusion of incompatibles is the root 'cause' of all our experience in the world, all our experience as apparently limited human beings, who say: 'I am, I think, I feel, I am alive.'

This mingling of consciousness and mind, of subject and object, of Self and not-Self, of the unchangeable and the transient, can only occur as a result of an error, of wrong knowledge, of something not being under-stood, of something essential about our nature not being realized. This error is what is described in the philosophy of Vedanta as false superimposition. It is at the core of our experience, and is what the Upanishads call 'the knot of the heart'. The error can only be dispelled through Self-knowledge in the deepest sense. That knowledge, indicated in the Upanishad, is summed up in the statement: 'I am Brahman', '*Aham Brahmasmi*'.

It was said earlier that, up to a certain point, we can work this out for ourselves. Our reason and discern-ment can attain a deep understanding of what we are not—of what our true 'I' cannot be identified with because it is an object of the I's awareness. But then we reach a point where our powers of reasoning and discrimination, unaided, will collapse and fail to make the final penetration into the true nature of the 'I'. We will need help if this mystery is to be solved.

The revealed scriptures of the Upanishads, mediated by the enlightened teacher, have as their ultimate aim the transmission of the highest truth—That which transcends reason and even transcends our highest speculations. The Upanishad awakens us to our true nature by reminding us: 'Thou art Brahman, That Thou Art. There is no other reality and reality is one without a second.' This supreme knowledge, this lamp of transcendent wisdom, is the light that dispels the dark illusion that covers the heart of humanity. For the fact is:

> Thou art that Brahman, free from all change, the same within and without, bliss absolute.

> *(Avadhut Gita, 1:14)*